CH00903755

Life of an

Endo Doll

Life of an Endo Doll

A few years ago, I started a blog. A blog that spiralled and was accessed daily by hundreds of women (and men) around the world, sometimes accidental, sometimes by fluke but mostly all were seeking help, seeking advice and seeking comfort in the knowledge that they were not the only one.

You see, I was fighting a condition called Endometriosis.

Endometriosis affects 1 in 10 women.

Every woman's endometriosis journey is different.

This is my story.

Chapter 1
In The Beginning

When I really look back my problems started way before I even started my periods. I remember being in hospital with suspected appendicitis at around 10 years old; it wasn't. I now know it was most likely Endometriosis as I was never treated for appendicitis but I do remember how they couldn't get to the bottom of my pain, so I was discharged from hospital with no answers. Before I started my periods I had many symptoms of Endometriosis in terms of lower abdomen pain. They were few and far between but they were never the typical childhood 'tummy aches' or 'stomach bugs'. I always remember this sharp tugging pain from my belly button right down towards the top of my vagina, as though someone had a tight, sharp elastic band that they were pulling and if I tried to stand up straight it would be impossible because the pain that would wash over me was so intense. I would have to bend over with my legs curled up into me until it disappeared. I recall my mother asking for a doctor to come out and see me on one occasion when this was happening, he put it down to a water infection without even testing my urine for an infection!

I'll never forget when I started my period for the first time. It's actually laughable now looking back as that very same day we had been given 'the talk' about periods at school, I think it must have been around October time as it was still quite warm. How ironic to start your periods on the day you have a talk about them! Of course when everyone was still talking about them the next day as young girls do after such a lesson and I said my first one had started the evening before, my school friends didn't believe me... well, would you? Of course that was the start of things to come as everything seemed to kick off pretty much straight away. I had intense period pains which of course when you complain of it hurting you are told 'are normal and something to get used to'. 'Have some paracetamol' became my mantra for many years, although of course it didn't really help.

In my first year of secondary school it was compulsory to do swimming every week, I think I must have been swimming three times in that first year... I really don't remember taking part that much. What I do remember is having a talk with two of my teachers discussing why I was yet again not going swimming, and I think it was the first time I had ever been in trouble in my whole school life! I recall feeling so upset and ashamed as I genuinely wanted to go swimming but how could I when I was always bleeding! I had been on my period for the second week running, so naturally the teachers thought I must have been acting up and making excuses so I didn't have to go swimming. I remember being told about using tampons so I could still attend swimming classes… No way! I was 12 years old I didn't want to use a tampon, they scared me (still do in fact!), and I just couldn't do it! When my mum took me to the doctors, the doctor just put it down to my cycle settling down and that it could just well be my menstrual cycle and something I'd just need to get used to. I remember that being the first of many visits to the doctor.

So my period hell continued, gradually getting worse as the years went by. I'd have them almost every two weeks, my head would spin, my vision would become blurry from the pain of it all, and I'd be doubled up in pain... no, not pain, that's the wrong word... agony. Sometimes I would be sick, faint and burst into tears for what seemed like no reason whatsoever. I was drained. It would interfere with my life, I couldn't go swimming with my friends, I didn't have the energy to go out and do anything. I didn't attend school when I should, I was constantly tired, sleeping in most days till late in the day, only turning up to school when I felt like I could; because of that my friendships weren't strong and my schoolwork started to slide. I'll never forget the time when my Mum came home from work; I was in so much pain that I was screaming on the floor doubled over. I felt so hot, I'd been sick, I could barely walk. My mum took me to the hospital to the A&E department. I was asked to do a urine sample and it was whilst I went to the bathroom that I realised I had started my period. I was 14. I was so embarrassed, I told Mum we had to leave immediately. She tried to get me to stay but I wasn't having any of it. I felt so ashamed and embarrassed that a period was causing this pain. I just wanted to go home and hide. If only I had stayed, perhaps I might have seen a doctor from the gynaecology department.

I wish I had stayed as the many different GP's I went to see was more than ridiculous. Going back and forth to see the doctors was in itself tiring as they constantly made you feel like you were just being a silly little girl, and obviously over reacting.

I was constantly told the following, time after time, repeatedly...

- It is normal to have periods that are heavy

- It is probably just your cycle why you have them every 2 weeks

- You have a low pain threshold compared to your friends

- You're not eating properly which is why you get dizzy

- It's all in your head

- You have Chronic Fatigue Syndrome

- You have IBS

- You have depression

- You are severely anaemic

- Oh it's nothing to worry about

- And again, it's normal.

I asked when I was 15 after doing some research online whether there was a chance I could have

Endometriosis (and I asked again at 18 to a different doctor) to be told, "No, it's all in your head, the pain is normal, you're too young. Don't use the internet to self-diagnose. Here are some anti-depressants, you have CFS". I KNEW what they were saying was wrong, but at 15 I didn't have the voice that I have now. You must understand that being repeatedly told that it's all in your head, that it's normal, time and time again and the way they SAY it... Oh it's so belittling. You feel so tiny and insignificant sat on that little chair next to their imposing desk and computer. To be laughed at by a doctor is horrible. How I wish I could meet every single one of those doctors I asked for help and tell them what happened to me!

I never did take those anti-depressants I was prescribed. My mum didn't pick the prescription up, knowing herself that that wasn't what was wrong with me, that something wasn't right but at a loss as to what to do next.

Over the years I've been prescribed a couple of different types of medication. I'm sure mostly just because they didn't have a clue what to do with me. If only I had known to ask for a referral to a gynaecologist! The first thing I was ever prescribed was something called 'mefenamic acid' which they say is to help reduce bleeding and pain. For me it was a waste of time, I was told to take it a few days before, during and after my period but with my periods every two weeks, how could I judge what day I would begin my period? It was just too much hard work and when I did manage to get the timings right it didn't do much for me anyway!

The next type of medication I was prescribed which I think is the most common, 'go to' medication to prescribe for any girl or woman coming to the GP with problems with their periods is the contraceptive pill. This one they'll prescribe so flippantly, like it's not an issue to have a tiny pill mess with your hormones. "Oh you don't want to be on it? Well there's nothing else we can do for you." So you feel you have no choice but to go on this nightmare of a pill. I was started on this having just turned 15, it was what the doctor said 'a low-dosage one' called Femodette. I stayed on this till I was 19, the most amazing thing about it was that it did help regulate my periods and my pain was reduced during the weeks I wasn't on my period.

Now the reason I call the contraceptive pill, 'a nightmare of a pill' is because at 19 it started causing me problems, I began with severe migraines. There was one occasion where I was at university and I almost fainted in the city centre and I actually went into the nearest opticians to have an eye test as I firmly believed there was something wrong with my eyes. It was there I found out that I was having focal migraines. Zig zag lines that would start across my eyes increasing in intensity till a full blown pounding headache would start and I would want to be sick. These would continue every month until eventually I went to the doctors and was told to come off the pill and when I asked "but what about my pain", then began the long road of trialling what felt like every contraceptive pill out there. Most causing horrific acne which by this point I had dropped out of university because I just couldn't focus on my degree due to the pain and fatigue I was experiencing. Instead I was working in cosmetics which is quite a tough job to be working in when you're suffering with acne and you're trying to sell makeup! Most would also cause more migraines, which in turn would interfere with my work life because the bright lights in the beauty hall would set off a migraine if it was around that time of the month but it also affected my social life! I would pass out on nights out or have to head home early because strobe lights would bring on a migraine and cause such intense pain I could barely stand.

I did eventually find one which was amazing, it was called Cerazette, and it actually stopped my periods completely. It was incredible for a while, despite still having the tiredness and aches and pains, I was in less pain as I was having no periods. This pill was the closest I got to feeling how I did pre-puberty. Again, that didn't last long as 6 months down the line, I had to stop taking it when I started with migraines again and I just couldn't be bothered anymore. All this faffing around trying different medication was frustrating. I was also becoming really pissed off with the fact my only option to try and be pain free was the contraceptive pill which didn't even work half the time. I came off everything when I was 21 and I've refused to be on the pill ever since.

Over the years I was also prescribed the anti-depressants I mentioned before, referred for counselling as I was most likely 'just depressed', co-codomol was also prescribed which was the strongest medication I had been offered to be taken when on my period alongside over the counter ibuprofen.

I stopped going to the doctors when I was around 21 years old as I was getting nowhere. No-one believed me, no-one was willing to help or listen. What was the point anymore?

I gave up.

Chapter 2
Getting a Diagnosis

I found a lump just after my 24th Birthday, on my lower left side of my abdomen. I thought fuck this, I'm not going to the doctors, waste of time, and they really don't care.

The lump gradually got bigger and I could feel it moving around.

I went to Japan on holiday to visit my cousin who lived out there at the time. I was incredibly exhausted the whole trip, I think my cousin has countless photographs of me fast asleep in various positions and scenic backgrounds! I remember him asking me if I was always this tired, I told him over the past year that I'd got gradually worse and it's probably just old age! I didn't think anything of it as I was so used to being so tired, I thought it was normal. I was embarrassed that I was always falling asleep so easily. The flight back from Japan was horrific. I had to change at Paris on the way back to Manchester and I remember being sick and being bent over double as I was just in so much pain! I put it down to just being tired from my trip and the long flight from Japan to Paris. When I got to Manchester I couldn't wait to get home, I could barely eat anything I felt so drained!

Months pass by and I'm beginning to stress about the lump I could feel, the pain getting worse and worse. I'm sure I could feel the lump moving when I walked or was it just in my head like all those doctors would surely tell me. It would bounce around and feel like it was pulling on something inside.

Each day starts to become a major struggle, I can barely open my eyes to get up for work so I start going to bed earlier to see if that helps. Until I wake up one morning screaming. I didn't realise I was already screaming, I had woken up in pain, shouting for my Mum. I couldn't move in my bed, I was trapped there. It felt as though the coils in the mattress had pierced through my body and pinned me to the bed and my lower half was encased in concrete. I was tensed up in so much pain and my bed sheets covered in blood, it was like I had had a haemorrhage in my sleep. My Mum had to swing my legs around and get me out of bed and help to clean me up. Later that day after numerous painkillers I had an appointment at the doctors.

When I get there, I have an examination and more swabs (which yes, you guessed it, came back negative a few weeks later as they had done for the past 12 years). To be told I am FINALLY being sent for an Ultrasound Scan! I was incredibly scared as I had been told it could be one of two things... but there is no point mentioning those but... Not ONCE was Endometriosis mentioned... despite having:

Painful periods

Pain during internal examinations

Pain during sex

Pelvic Pain

Heavy periods with clots

Excessive bleeding

Irregular periods

Loss of old 'dark' blood

Depression

Back Pain

Excessive fatigue

Leg pains

Oh and the big fuck off lump in my abdomen near my left ovary.

I mentioned every single one of the above as I have done for years, plus a few others to do with the bowel area... and ridiculously Endometriosis wasn't mentioned. The ignorance of some medical staff still amazes me now, for something as COMMON and as far as I'm concerned something everyone should know about... I mean... I KNEW ABOUT IT AT 15 YEARS OLD. It took one search on Google with a couple of my symptoms for Endometriosis to come up... so why can't a PROFESSIONAL know of Endo?

It FRUSTRATES me so much.

I go home, as I am to now wait for a letter, having been told it would take 5-6 weeks to come through. In the meantime, the pain has increased, I'm getting more and more exhausted by the day and I just can't cope. I'm so done with having to push past this pain now. You get used to it over the years but this is too much, enough is enough, I need help! One morning I get in so much pain, I have to ring in work again to say I'm going to be late because I'm going to the doctors this morning. I go to the doctor's, except this time I have purposely asked to see a specific doctor at the surgery. I have never seen them before but after reading on the surgery's website about their team, this particular doctor says she has a special interest in women's health. I thought this would finally be my answer to GP's wasting my time and treating me like my pain is insignificant. I had finally got an appointment with a GP who had an interest in women's health; surely she would know and not dismiss me! I explain my situation, AGAIN, so tired of repeating myself when surely everything is right there on my records. Her diagnosis…

Food poisoning.

Yeah… funny isn't it. I guess you could mis-diagnose intense abdominal pain, diarrhoea, dizziness, bleeding, fatigue and a lump as food poisoning. I can totally understand. Seriously. Considering I'd eaten the exact same food as my Mum the previous day and she was absolutely fine. Laugh out loud funny.

So I head to work, I do my shift and then BAM! The pain is ridiculously high. I can take pain but I couldn't handle this. This was so intense I could barely breathe. I managed to pick up the phone and ring my Dad, he rings his fiancée and she rushes to pick me up from work. Taking me straight to the A&E room at Stepping Hill Hospital as I had bleeding and ridiculous pain, struggling to walk the pain was so intense. Yet again, I explain my situation to the triage nurse and how I'm awaiting an ultrasound scan blah blah blah. The triage nurse says, 'This is not food poisoning' and looked quite annoyed, maybe angry when she said that. I get to see a doctor quite quickly, which was amazing for a Thursday evening in A&E. Oh but the doctor I saw in A&E... I wish I could thank her over and over and over and over and over and over and over and... you get the picture.

After describing my symptoms and what has been happening the FIRST words out of her mouth are, 'this sounds like Endometriosis', and 'this sounds like an Endometriotic Cyst'. I could have kissed her, I started crying, finally there was someone that was on the same wavelength as me, someone who knew what they were talking about. I'm so happy at being told this news which sounds incredibly odd I know! But 12 years of not knowing, not being heard, not being listened to, it was like a huge weight had been lifted off my shoulders. So much relief, I wasn't insane, it wasn't in my head. This professional thinks there IS something wrong with me; she thinks it IS potentially endometriosis. The one thing I had asked about 9 years previous. Happy, so happy but then the fear set in. What would happen now?

I get sent home with painkillers and told I am to have a scan early next morning back at the hospital and that it would have been done then but the ultrasound department was closed. I go home to bed as it's so late and I try not to worry.

I ring up in the morning to find out what time my scan will be. I'm told to start drinking water as my scan is first on the list at 8am. I'm struggling to drink enough water but I manage it, it hurts so much having my bladder so full that I can barely walk. We get to the hospital for my scan. I'm to go up to Jasmine Suite; if only I knew then that's where I would be spending the next two years. I'm asked to lie on the bed as the sonographer applies some super cold jelly to my lower abdomen. She starts to move the device around my belly, all I can see is black and tiny fragments of whitish grey here and there. Calmly she tells me that the big dark shadow I can see on the screen is an Endometriotic cyst, otherwise known as a chocolate cyst as it is filled with blood. The panic starts to set in, it really is Endometriosis. I'm told I haven't drank enough water (I drank over a litre of water that morning, like they had asked!) so I then had to have a Transvaginal Scan, I had to sign a little form agreeing to this and wow it was scary! The device looked like E.T's finger, sorry, it's just what it reminded me of. It scared the hell out of me and all I wanted to do was cry and I did when I got told about the size of my cyst. The blood filled cyst was measuring roughly around 8cm big. I then find out there are others on the opposite side but ones I don't have to worry about.

I then had to wait for the consultant I have now been allocated to have a quick look and decide what he thinks. I get put into a little room to wait with my Mum whilst I cry because I'm scared. I have never had an operation in my life and by then of course, I pretty much figured they were going to have to get it out! I was petrified. At this point, the fact that I had been told it was Endometriosis, still hadn't sunk in. And I still didn't really understand what that meant for me.

Patiently waiting.

Chapter 3

Where was I? Oh yes... the waiting room. This is where I now meet my consultant, who I must stress right now is absolutely FANTASTIC!

He introduces himself, tells me he will need to operate and remove it. Speaks to me briefly about my symptoms and tells me it is quite a sizeable Endometriotic Cyst and it must go! I am then prescribed some painkillers and he tells me I need to attend his next clinic session to discuss what I have and all my options. He insists that I must write down any questions no matter how small and bring them with me to my appointment.

In the meantime whilst I am waiting to attend his discussion session, I go back to work as normal, carry on as normal, the pain getting progressively worse and worse.

A letter comes through from my GP to say I have to attend an Ultrasound Scan, I call them and say it's too late I've already had one at the hospital plus a Transvaginal Scan.

I get my appointment through to see my consultant, and he explains all about Endometriosis to me and what he's going to do to remove the cyst. I remember crying a lot during my discussion with him, I think it was a combination of fear and relief. To know that I wasn't a crazy/hypochondriac (and that there really was something wrong) that I wasn't just making things up like I had been led to feel over the years by different doctors. There really was something wrong. I get prescribed more painkillers and I am now to await a letter for scans and pre-op.

I'm not sure of the exact dates/timings but I'm going to take a guess at a few weeks later. I get in huge amounts of pain at work towards the end of my shift and I look down and I have begun to bleed. I was bleeding so much that it was running down my leg in my tights. I was so ashamed and embarrassed and I didn't know what to do. I stood behind my till (I work in cosmetics retail) and waited for 8pm to arrive. In the meantime, I rang my Dad and told him whilst trying not to cry, he told me he was on his way. Every minute felt like an hour, when in reality it was only 20 minutes or so. I manage to get out of work whilst crying my eyes out the moment I left the shop floor; holding onto the wall whilst I made my way out. My floor manager helped me to the Security Lodge and sat me down and made sure I was okay until my Dad arrived. I was so scared and embarrassed, it's times like those that I wish I had a job where I could sit down and hide under a table!

I get to the A&E department and get the joy of sitting and watching the Opening of the Olympics. Although I missed the point where our lovely Queen jumped out of the helicopter as I was having a blood test! I got sent for the blood test quite quickly and given some Oramorph and some other painkillers, can't remember what though! Short time later I am seen by a gynaecologist with a lovely Scottish accent. Not sure why that's relevant but it's what I remember! Obviously by this point I can hardly feel anything I'm so medicated. Add to that the fact I hadn't eaten anything, I was pretty spaced out. He asks me a few questions, like where my pain is etc, and asks me to rate my pain on the 1-10 scale. Keeping in mind when I got there it was a good 100. I tell him, 'Oh, it's alright, I'm fine now'. My Mum explaining to me it's because I'd just had some Oramorph and it's masking whatever pain I do have. He lies me down and examines my belly and as soon as he touches my left side I am crying out in pain and there are tears streaming down my face. Within a few minutes, he's got me in a wheelchair and is admitting me to the Jasmine Suite in the Women's Unit on the other side of the hospital.

The last time I spent the night in hospital was when I was 10? Oh and that was with suspected appendicitis. So anyway, I'm scared and when I get up there it's now 1am? My Mum in this time (I remember having to wait for a while for a bed to be set up for me), had driven home and packed me a bag of overnight things. I was wheeled upstairs to the ward and taken into a 4 bed room with a little light on in the corner next to a window, with my name above the bed. A lovely student nurse came to sign all the forms with me and made sure I was okay. I said goodbye to my Mum and then had a little cry!

I hadn't paid my phone bill so I couldn't text or ring anyone, so frustrating.

The lovely student nurse comes back in and tells me I'm nil by mouth and to make myself comfortable. I am to wait for the Dr who had seen me in A&E; he had just gone to do a Caesarean which was why there was a slight wait. I drifted off to sleep and when I woke at 2am the student nurse and this Dr was round my bed, he was explaining how I was to be nil by mouth all night as there is a strong possibility they would have to operate in a few hours as he feared the Endo cyst had wrapped itself around my ovary. He did a quick examination of my belly and told me he didn't want to do an internal as I was clearly in a lot of pain and he didn't want to make things worse for me. Which I really appreciated!

I drift off to sleep and before I know it, it's 7am and the same student nurse has asked me if I want a bit of toast as the Dr had decided against surgery and wants me to have an Ultrasound scan and an MRI scan. I was so relieved that I wasn't having emergency surgery and he must have been satisfied with me going to sleep that the cyst hadn't wrapped itself around my ovary. Good news.

I have an Ultrasound Scan later that day, and good news... (can I call it that?) The cyst is still there in the same position but is bigger than the first scan I had a few weeks ago and takes up the majority of the screen.

I then spend a week on the lovely Jasmine Suite with some of the most caring and supportive nurses I've ever met. I have an MRI Scan in that time, and that week I am almost pain free as my pain is so well managed. I wish it could be like that all the time!

I think I will leave it there for now. So much more to say before I get to the present day, which I hope to get to quite soon as I really want to talk about my next appointments. That's if you're still enjoying reading this. If not it's okay, I'll still be here blabbering on about myself.

Chapter 4
More of Getting Diagnosed…

I'd just spent a week in hospital, and when I get home my pain becomes sky high again. It takes a few more days to get in under control again. It's a few weeks later when I have to go back to get my results although most of my timings are guesswork.

I go back to the hospital when my appointment date comes through and I see my consultant, who is once again, amazing! So understanding and sympathetic. He explains to me he will be doing surgery to remove the Endo Cysts and excise the Endometriosis, he explains he has placed my Endo at around a Stage Three but it will be confirmed once I've had surgery. Excise means to cut away and when done by a skilled surgeon can be very effective. He goes on to explain the levels of Endo they use at the hospital and it goes from One to Four. He also explains that someone with Stage One Endo can have excruciating pain and someone with Stage Four may have little pain. He tells me it's a system they use for the amount of Endo present; it is not a pain scale.

He explains he will do a test to check my fallopian tubes where they place dye into the tubes as he knows that one day I'd like to try for a baby. He also explains as my left ovary is so enlarged he will pin it up to give it a rest with stitches that dissolve. And if when he gets in there he will have to remove my left ovary but only if it is causing damage to my body but he will do his best to preserve it.

Now all I have to do is wait for a date for my surgery and then attend a pre-op session.

During this time I'd been dating this amazing man, who was really supportive and had even gone online to research what Endometriosis was which REALLY amazed me. I mean the majority of guys would have done one or just pretended they were bothered but not gone out of their way to understand it. Before this I'd been on a few (okay quite a lot, I like free food haha) dates with other guys but ending up ignoring them and carried on dating this guy. I think it was a combination of his genuine caring personality and the fact he made me laugh. I needed that. Still do!

Again, fast forward to my pre-op. For anyone out there who is about to have surgery or has never had surgery. It's basically just a bunch of questions like, 'Is there a chance you could be pregnant? Doubt it, I'm virtually infertile', 'Do you smoke?', 'Have you been ill lately' etc etc. And then they take a whole heap of blood off you, check your blood pressure and your heart rate. Nothing to worry about and the nurse made you feel at ease.

I've got to stress before all these hospital appointments I was PETRIFIED of needles. They don't bother me anymore I've been prodded with them that much, I've had to get used to them.

So far so good.

Progression.

Chapter 5
First Surgery

My surgery date comes through, I have to take a bowel prep the day before... this was oh wow... V I L E. Only way to describe it! You drink this stuff and I swear make sure you have another drink to drink straight after and whatever you do, don't smell it as it will make you gag! Make sure you have some good reading material as you'll be in the bathroom all day. The next day, I'm up at 6 to be at the hospital for 7am. Now, for an operation you're not allowed to wear makeup. THIS was the worst part of my day. I LOVE my makeup; it makes me feel so much better and confident. When I don't wear it, I don't feel like myself. But I managed to get away with my eyebrow make-up. I don't think they noticed as they said nothing about it! Bonus for me, I know it sounds crazy but it made me feel a little less nervous!

The guy I had been dating for the previous few months, was by now all official and we're still together now! He sent me into hospital with this little toy monkey who I call Mali Bu Bu and a box of Lucky Charms. He's the best boyfriend ever!

My Mum takes me up to the ward and by coincidence I'm in the exact same bed as when I spent a week in hospital, which was good, it made me feel a bit more relaxed. Again, I'm probably sounding crazy there!

I'm the second op of the day, and I get taken down at 8am. I walked down to the operating theatre area, you get checked in and they ask you questions and you lie down on an allocated bed. Wearing the oh so attractive hospital gown. They also gave me a magazine to read whilst I was waiting to have my anaesthetic, although I didn't read it as I was too scared! The words blurred before my eyes.

A few minutes later, I'm wheeled into the anaesthetic room before I go into theatre. The lovely man there puts a cannula into my hand and then he says to me, I'm just going to put something in your hand to numb it and then after that I can't remember a thing!

Next thing I remember is waking up screaming in the recovery room because I was in pain and I felt all strange. I just remember someone smiling at me and putting something in the cannula and then waking up in the lift back up to the ward and I start asking if I can have a Nando's. God knows why!

I then drift off back to sleep and next wake up when my Mum is there half an hour later at visiting time and I wake up to her laughing. I ask her what she's laughing at and she says the fact I was asking for a Nando's and if I'm still hungry? I was like NO! I feel BLAH, I can't eat!

Later that evening, my consultant comes round and explains to me what he's done and what he's found. He removed the cysts and explained the one that was attached to my left ovary was 15cm around and there was a lot more endo there than what he could see on the scans. Obviously he excised the majority of this! He had also discovered a lot of scar tissue, endo on the surface of my bladder and bowel, almost pinning them together. He said he couldn't excise this as there was too much of a risk of ending up with a colostomy bag and other complications. So he wants to speak to another doctor about putting a stent in my water pipe to see the endo better and he wants to discuss a plan for me as we both didn't know about the endo being there before he operated and we hadn't discussed it. He didn't want to do any surgery that we hadn't discussed.

I'm also glued, not stitched which was weird to see. I also had a 4th hole rather than the 3 that I was expecting which was a bit of a shock but I got over it. After all, it's removed that huge 15cm endo cyst, no wonder I had customers asking me if I was pregnant! My belly was huge before the op, and at this point it still is. I can only recommend a hell of a lot of Peppermint Tea. It is absolutely amazing for getting rid of the gas from the surgery.

One down.

Chapter 6

My recovery went well, I think it helped that I was glued rather than stitched. Although my belly button is still healing now, months on which is a bit worrying but oh well. At the end of October 2012, I started Prostap, the chemically induced menopause. This involves monthly injections over 6 months. The main purpose is to stop my periods and get rid of the pain and shrink the Endometriosis. Side effects that I have had with this are:

Hot flushes

Major depression

Emotions completely unstable

Weight Gain... I've put a stone on since I started these injections. I don't know whether anyone else has found this? It would be great to know as this is just adding to my depression!

Lots of tiredness, I love a nap

Increased pain

Backache has got worse

Memory is all over the place

So yeah... things were supposed to get better but they're not. Oh I've also had random bleeding. Since the end of October I've been going back and forth to have these injections. They are always in my belly whether it's on the left or the right and only once has it hurt. I tend to get a rash around the area for a few days and a swelling, but if I massage the swelling even though it's tender, it does help it to go down.

Oh and the side effects they don't tell you about are:

Hair gets dry

Skin goes mental

And both of these are important to me, working in cosmetics I need smooth soft hair. I've recently started a shed load of hair oil treatments as my hair has been falling out constantly.

I'm finding this treatment incredibly difficult. From what I've read online, most women react great to it and found it really helped them, but for me things are getting worse. In particular the being really depressed side of things. I keep telling myself it will all be over soon but every time I go back to the hospital, it seems more and more things are showing up.

Menopausal 25 Year Old.

Fun Times.

Chapter 7
My latest hospital appointment

This was the reason why I wanted to start writing. Tuesday was a really long tiring day for me at the hospital and I just felt like I couldn't take any more of this absolute crap and I had to get this started and just write it all out of me. And you know what, it's helped! Just to know that there are all you Endosisters are reading this too. It makes me feel like I'm not alone. At the same time, it makes me feel sad that so many of us have it. In the past month, since me speaking to people about my symptoms and how I eventually got diagnosed, three of my friends have been diagnosed with Endometriosis. Now I'm not saying every woman out there has it. Because it's absolutely NOT the case. But wow, if I'm giving other women the courage to demand more opinions at the GP's then I feel like I'm giving something back. For the past year, I've been online reading blogs, reading forums, reading posts on twitter but never really commenting, just staying quiet and you've all helped me so much. I just hope that my writing is now helping others, the way yours has helped me.

So my latest hospital appointment, I'd had an MRI scan a few weeks ago and I received the results on Tuesday. Basically my left ovary hasn't gone back to 'normal', I now have endo on my right ovary, my central line, my uterus is over to the left and is an abnormal shape, and the endo that was on the surface of my bowel last time? It looks as though it has gone through my bowel wall and is a 2cm circumference so far, which is manageable if it doesn't grow any bigger. I also have something on my fallopian tube that looks like the beginnings of endo on the left.

My consultant asked me if I'd been having pain on my right side, I said yes and that I found it unusual as usually it's only now and again that I get pain there but recently I'd been getting masses of pain every day.

The fact that the endo has got worse and the uterus is over to the left explains why my bladder and bowel are now so close together.

I also had some extra scans done on Tuesday to help with research amongst the doctors at the hospital, which I really don't mind doing. But by the end of the day I was so tired, so tired of being prodded and by that point in so much pain and all I wanted to do was go jump off a bridge somewhere. And I'm not saying that flippantly, I think this Prostap is really affecting me.

I now have to wait for an appointment to come through to see my consultant's other doctor. I have to have a test done where I have a bowel prep, I have dye put in my bowel and a camera put up there. They have measured it at around 17cm up. It is called a Barium Enema.

What I'd really, really, like to know... is there anyone who's reading this that has had this done? I'm scared and I don't know what to expect, I'm being sedated but it's not the point. I like to know every little detail, I find it helps me.

Just as I thought things were getting better and this menopause treatment has to be the future... bang, my body thinks "No chance honey, let's attack you with some more endo, you can take the pain!"

And I can't anymore, I really can't. I'm sick and tired of putting a brave face on for work and smiling all day when all I want to do is go home, cry and sleep the pain off. I think I'd find it easier if I had a job where I could sit down. I can't, I stand and walk around all day. Got to make money though haven't we!

I'm just so thankful to have an amazing, caring, supportive boyfriend. And the best Mum in the world, she's been there for me every step of the way, always on the end of the phone if I need to talk; always helping me with new treatments I can try, like gluten-free diets and that type of thing. She is my absolute rock. If it wasn't for them, I just wouldn't see the point in getting out of bed in the morning right now.

I will be more positive soon, I'm sure.

Waiting for my appointment…and some advice!

Chapter 8
This weekend... 5th Prostap Kicking In

Ahh where to begin? The past few days have been incredibly up and down for me! On Friday, I had a day off from work and I thought, 'Great! I can look after my boyfriend'. He had an operation last Monday to fix a sports injury (he's a professional rugby player), and I thought, 'Yes, perfect girlfriend, Friday can be the day I can give him a 110% attention.' Uh uh, didn't work out that way did it, stupid fucking Endo got in the way. As per usual whenever I want to do something with my time off.

Latest prostap injection kicked in hard on Friday and my emotions were all over the show, talk about Drama Queen! I was in a really emotional state, tried doing the washing up, pain kicked in ended up leaving the majority of it so the kitchen now looked like an absolute mess, which ANNOYS me. I like things to be clean and tidy! And it's not like my boyfriend could do anything as he was under strict orders from his consultant not to lift anything or do anything for 12 days. Not even a kettle! So had a bitch fit about the fact that I was in pain, had a lie down, felt like crap and then got overly emotional and felt like a shocking girlfriend because I couldn't do anything for my boyfriend, getting upset and thinking stuff like, 'Oh my god, you're injured, I'm supposed to be the one to look after you and I can't do anything because of this ridiculous illness, wish it would just fuck off'. Of course my boyfriend wasn't bothered about the washing up, but it wasn't just that it was the fact I just didn't have the energy to get up, make him food and drinks and stuff. All the things that I would be doing if I wasn't feeling the way I was!

Honestly, the smallest things were really getting to me on Friday. I then spent about 4 hours in the angriest mood for no reason whatsoever! I couldn't shake it off. I was annoyed about everything and anything.

My boyfriend was the one who ended up looking after ME on Friday and I just felt so bad because it should have been the other way around. He's so bloody amazing!

Saturday… I woke up exhausted and in agony, took me an hour to get out of bed but I made it to work and got there early, bonus! Had a brilliant day in work despite being in a lot of pain all day but you just have to grin and bear it. I'm dealing with customers all day long and there's no time to feel sorry for yourself, just have to slap a smile on and get on with it. Anyway, I'd smashed my target for the month and so had our counter. So I was really happy with this. Add to that I'd had a really nice customer compliment that week and I'd had recognition from both my floor manager and my manager for this. It was a great day in work.

I then went to my Dad's for tea and whilst I was waiting for my Dad to get home from work I was having a chat with his fiancée and at one point got all emotional and had a little cry... AGAIN. Just about everything I'd found out on Tuesday. It's only really just hitting me how much worse my Endo has got... for it to be now on my right ovary, left fallopian tube and blah blah. I guess

I genuinely believed the prostap would shrink everything. Oh well, c'est la vie.

I wake up this morning, still tired and in pain. I have some great painkillers but I don't take them regularly as I'm scared I'm going to end up relying on them. I'm trying to reduce pain with the types of food that I eat and my way of thinking. Which I know is probably silly of me but I have an addictive personality and if I start knocking back Tramadol all day long, I know it will be hard for me to come off them! I took Teddy (our puppy) on a long walk with my boyfriend's Mum and his Gran and he had the best time ever and I was feeling good, not in too much pain.

Chapter 9

I have been extremely poorly and just haven't had the energy to do anything, let alone write. I've also recently spent a week in hospital but more on that soon!

My appointment came through to see another consultant. A specialist with the bowel area (I have NO IDEA what the real term is...); I absolutely panicked as I hadn't received any medication or anything, as I fully presumed this would be the scan date. Uh uh, I was wrong, a few days later, my Mum calls to say I've had a letter and in it is my medication and a further appointment date. So that must be the second appointment.

I go along to this appointment to meet the consultant and it's not like the women's unit where everyone knows you on a first name basis and everything's light and friendly. It's all small rooms, and small waiting area and I feel very nervous! Eventually, after what felt like a century, I was called through and put into a room. I was expecting an office, like when I go and see my gynae consultant. NO! Just a bed, light... etc it was basically an examination room. At this point, I'm full on scared as I can now deal with things in the vagina area, but not THAT area, no-one's ever been there before!

The consultant comes in and he's lovely, I like him straight away. He explains what's going to happen and what they are looking for and again explains to me that my surgery will be a joint operation with both him and my gynae consultant operating on me. I guess it's a bit like when you go to the hairdressers and you have two people doing your hair sometimes!

I was always under the impression that both types of scan would be on the same day, but apparently not. The scan I will be having the following week will be the Barium Enema. And then I will be having a type of Endoscopy (can't remember the name, I will find out when I have it) where he will be performing this scan and placing a camera into my larger bowel to find the Endometriosis.

It was quite a short brief meeting, but I presume it was just so I could meet him first and if I had any questions I could ask him there and then. He also asked me to lie on the bed facing the wall, with my knees bent and then he did an internal examination to check whether he could find anything abnormal. Which he couldn't. Which is great, but we all know the Endometriosis is around 17cm into my bowel but I'm glad nothing else sinister is going on!

Wow. Brief meeting over. And the sooner all these scans are done with the BETTER. As I am NOT happy with being prodded and poked about anyway but especially not in that area. Like, I genuinely hate it; it is so embarrassing I think I can deal with the vagina area a lot more. As I've had examinations there since I was 8 years old and it's pretty much normal, you know!

Embarrassing!

Chapter 10
Ended Up In Hospital...

So I ended up talking about my appointment and didn't mention that the previous night I had attended A&E with my Dad and my Step-Mum because my pain had become so severe, I just couldn't move. A&E provided me with some pain relief – even though I have enough pain relief for a war zone, and they wanted to admit me to a ward. I flat out refused and said I'm seeing a doctor tomorrow anyway about my next operation. I just need you to get rid of my pain. So they helped and said, if it gets worse to come straight back.

I kept fighting it for most of the week, Tuesday was obviously my appointment day and Wednesday I was on a late shift at work. That was a really hard day for me, I was in so much pain it was unbearable but I just tried to crack on the best I could. Thursday was my day off, my pain was up and down, and it's easier to take my medication at home. I can keep alarms on my phone and I have my boyfriend to remind me when I need to take my tablets. We took our puppy to Pets At Home and bought him a new bed, which he absolutely loves by the way! I also had a delivery arrive from boohoo.com (love this clothing website!) So I'm in all my new clothes looking amazing, I sit down after putting Teddy in his new bed so he can try it out. My boyfriend is in the kitchen making me a drink and then BAM! Tears just started flooding down my face and I'm screaming in pain.

I'd just like to point out that when this happens you know my pain is intense. I can hack a 9 on the ridiculous 1-10 scale, I can work on a 9. I've had years of coping with unexplained pain, and now I know what the pain is I know I can handle most of it. I call the 1-10 scale ridiculous... because how can you measure Endo pain? It can fluctuate like contractions!

My boyfriend starts panicking and I tell him to call my Mum, my Mum says to him to take me to A&E. We get to A&E within an hour (we live some distance away now; I refused to change hospitals as my doctor is amazing). I get to see a gynae doctor by around half 10, which wasn't too bad, I refused to have blood tests etc as I'd had all these done on Monday night. And I also know what the issue is. I got to see a gynae doctor and she had copies of some of my notes in front of her and said right, we're putting you onto Jasmine Ward. We're going to get some pain management sorted for you as what you're on right now, clearly isn't doing the job.

I spent a week on Jasmine Ward. Speaking to my EndoSisters on Twitter, updating photo's on Instagram. Just to keep my mind busy. I became seriously low in hospital to the point where yet again, I was feeling suicidal and I just couldn't cope. There were times when the Oramorph wasn't working and I just wanted to die. I couldn't take the pain. I don't want to deal with it. I don't see why I should have to deal with it. We need a cure. I couldn't be arsed fighting anymore.

The nurses and doctors were lovely, aside from one who said, 'Having a baby is the best thing for Endometriosis'... Oh piss off! Don't even get me started lady!

I had many scans whilst I was in there and there was an episode where I heard my amazing doctor get angry! Well, not angry... just annoyed! Basically the Ultrasound unit wouldn't scan me as my bladder wasn't full. I was down there and I suggested they just do a Transvaginal Scan as that's what they usually have to do as my bladder won't get full because of Endo. No they wouldn't do it, and then she started saying how my Barium Enema scan would have to be re-arranged so I could have this Ultrasound scan. That was it. After she disappeared back into the little office, I broke down in tears. I've waited for months for this Barium Enema and there was no way it was being cancelled now for a fucking Ultrasound scan. You can fuck right off. I was so stressed out. Also doesn't help I was in a waiting area where all these pregnant women are walking around, and my belly was so bloated, one woman said to me, 'Is this your first scan?' and I just burst into tears. Don't understand why she asked that when she could clearly see I was an in-patient as I was in my pyjamas and I had a hospital band around my wrist! Don't open your mouth! I guess some people just don't think.

I was taken back up to the ward and I just lay on my bed crying. Within a few seconds one of the ward nurses was giving me a hug and I explained what had happened and what the nurses down there were trying to do. She disappeared and within a few minutes, my doctor was at my bed telling me that my scan tomorrow is still going ahead and that I was to drink my Fleet and that later on this evening after he finishes for the day, he will do my scan himself.

He ended up doing a Transvaginal scan and it showed that I've had a cyst that looks as though it's popped as there is a lot of fluid behind my left ovary, which looked polycystic on the scan, also a mass of Endo behind my womb and on my bowel. Usual stuff, aside from that fluid. Blah blah. Not a lot had changed. Good sign. Still in agony. Also it was an incredibly painful examination, and I did cry a few times during but I soldiered through it.

Jeeez... this post is going to be a long one... I could break it up but, I'll just tell you about the Barium Enema. As I couldn't find an account of this anywhere online. I wanted to find a real account not something off an NHS website that only gives you the basics and makes it out to not be as bad as it sounds.

IT'S HORRIBLE. I HATED EVERY SECOND OF IT.

I cried before I even went in, just because I was so scared and didn't have a clue what was going to happen as my information guide was at home. I hadn't eaten for 48 hours so I was damn emotional. I like my food. The women that work down there are so amazing and have beautiful personalities. I had to go into a room and take off all my underwear and pants and put a hospital gown on which felt thicker than other ones I've worn before. I then had to come into the X-Ray room that had a kind of straight bed and loads of surrounding big futuristic equipment around it.

Because I was so nervous, they sat me down on the bed and explained everything to me and showed me everything that would happen. They have to stand behind a screen like in a normal X-Ray room whilst they take pictures. But obviously this one is different, I'd had to take Fleet the day before and empty my bowels. I also didn't agree with the Fleet at all, and had a night of horrendous pain, being sick, passing out on the ward floor. I hated every minute of it.

So I lie down on the bed facing the crazy, futuristic machinery and they basically insert a tube into my back passage *cringe* and it hurts! But nothing an EndoSister can't handle! You have to pretty much clench so it stays in and they then start to pump liquid into you so that it coats your bowel and intestines so it shows on the pictures. They then check to see that enough liquid is coating your insides and then they come and remove the majority of the liquid. Think of it like you put glue on a picture, shake glitter all over it and then tap the excess off!

They then start to bring this huge circular scan thing down so it's really close to your body and it takes pictures of your insides. The nurses then come and help you move into different positions; on your other side, on your back, on your belly, hips tilted etc. And there's also a moment where the bed tips upside down for a few moments and then tilts you back up vertically and back down again and then they take more pictures. There was a brief moment where I could see the screens and I could see what they were taking photos of but to be honest, I didn't have a clue what I was looking at so I didn't bother too much with that.

They then begin to pump air into you. Now this is the bit that I found so unbearable. It hurt. All this liquid and air was irritating my Endometriosis and it was so painful. I'm going to describe it as though someone had poured salt and lemon into an open wound. It was intense and agonising. I couldn't cope and was breathing heavily and crying in pain for the final 10 minutes.

Afterwards they take you to the toilet and you sort yourself out. Everything comes out pure white! It's kind of crazy. I know most of you probably don't want to know about all this, but hey, it's here for the EndoSisters that have to have this done as it's spread to these organs. You don't have to read this!

On the way back in the wheelchair, I was crying and just telling my Mum (who had come to the scan with me) that I just wanted this to be over and that I don't want to fight any more and I wanted a new body. Every depressing thought was escaping my mouth and I couldn't stop crying. The pain was just far too much for me to handle, on top of the fact I hadn't eaten.

The nurses that were on weren't that helpful when I got back though, they just said 'Well, it's your Endometriosis' and just shrugged their shoulders and that just really fucking irritated me (and my Mum). They gave me painkillers and my Doctor wanted me to stay in but I said no, I want to get rid of this pain and in the morning I want to go home.

So that's exactly what happened. I was discharged and signed off work for a minimum of 2 weeks as I wasn't fit for work because of the amount of painkillers... Tramadol, Naproxen, Codeine and Oramorph. Not to mention an antibiotic I now have to take for an infection I've picked up in hospital!

I'm back at the hospital next Tuesday for my Prostap injection which is my final one! I'm waiting for an appointment to come through for my Endoscopy thing, it does have another name but I can't remember what it is called! And then after that I will be awaiting my surgery date and having the joint operation.

Never-Ending.

Chapter 11
Still off work...

So I'm at home and I feel like I'm going crazy because I'm off work. I know I can't go back yet... doctor's orders. And even if I was to go back early then I know I'll just end up coming home because my pain still isn't under control and that is no good for the business. I can only go back to work when I'm almost 100%, when my pain is under control and well managed and I know I'm not going to have episodes of pain whilst working. I don't know whether that will be fully achieved till after my operation but I plan on trying to get it under control by next week.

I had a hospital appointment yesterday for my final Prostap injection (YES!)... And was told to wait back in the waiting area. Whilst she (one of my allocated nurses who works closely alongside my doctor) tracked down the date for my Sigmoidoscopy (that was the name that I couldn't remember from last time), as I still hadn't heard anything.

Whilst I was waiting for her to chase up my appointment date, my consultant and the radiographer came down to prepare for clinic starting at 2pm. I need to point out, because I'm there so often they let me go at half 1 to have my injection and if the doctors are there then I see them early.

The radiographer (I think that's what she is, probably something else though) is lovely, she is the doctor that did some research on me using Transvaginal

Ultra Sound Scan. She wanted to learn to spot the signs of Endometriosis on the scan. She was the doctor who did my MRI scan so she knew where my Endo was and she wanted to see if it was possible to pick it up on the scan, like they have been doing in the rest of Europe. This is the one where my consultant came and sat in on the scan and examined me at the same time too. Anyway, she spotted me and said hello and made a joke about me being here more than she is and she works there!

My consultant waved at me whilst he was taking a call and then went into his office and a few minutes later, my nurse called me in and said he wanted to see me.

He was going through my Barium Enema scan results, and it's not good. I've got Endometriosis in my Sigmoid colon and it has narrowed my bowel... ahh this is where I need to draw a picture! I wonder whether he will allow me to take a photo of my scan so I can show you all! On either side of each wall, endometriosis is attached and gone right through the bowel wall, and if you think of it like two trees touching each other to create an archway... then that's what is going on right there! I've also got endometriosis elsewhere in my bowel, but I can't remember what area he called that.

He said that research has proven that removing parts of the bowel in young people causes more problems later in life and is just not worth doing. He doesn't want to see me with a bag for example. Ideally he wants to shave off the Endometriosis away from my bowel and then stitch it back up. I'm not sure of everything yet as on Thursday (tomorrow) he will be discussing me in MDT – a monthly meeting to discuss Endometriosis patients and their care plans. And he will be deciding along with everyone else, how extensive my surgery needs to be. As I have endo underneath my water pipe and some on my bladder... not even mentioning the Endo that has grown since I started Prostap and has spread over my pelvic area again. Anyway, I'm now waiting for my Sigmoidoscopy as I have a date for it, but my consultant isn't happy with the date and wants me to have it in the next week.

He explained that the surgeon who will be operating on the bowel area is an extremely skilled surgeon, and he deals largely with cancer patients. I said to him, so because of Cancer Pathway my appointment has been pushed back a bit... which is fine, I certainly don't want people to die! I'm glad that it works like that, what I'm experiencing is nothing compared to them! My consultant said, well it's not fine, just because your disease isn't going to kill you, doesn't mean you can't have fast treatment. So now he is going to be speaking to the other surgeon to get my appointment much sooner, and before he goes on holiday. As my consultant wants to be operating on me in April/beginning of May.

He also wants me to see the Pain Management team again and up my painkillers as they're still not working effectively. So I'm waiting for an appointment to come through for that. He also told me that if I get in any pain and I can't control it, to come straight back in so they can get me up to speed with my pain management.

I did tell him that since the Barium scan, for a few days after it makes everything white when you go to the toilet, which is strange but it's the liquid they use you see. I told him that I've never noticed it before because I never look but I did this time just because I'd been told everything would be white, so I had a peek (vile, I know), but I noticed there were patches of blood. He told me this complicates things, which is why I need to have this Sigmoidoscopy to find out exactly how the Endo is and specifically where. He doesn't want to just go straight in and operate. Too many complications.

Yeah, so I'm not looking forward to this surgery. Stent in my water pipe. Ovaries suspended again. Bowel reconstruction (worst case scenario), lots and lots of excision. Very scared about this one to be honest. Not going to lie and say I'm fine!

Would like to be normal and back at work!

Chapter 12

As a lot of you know (because I speak to you via Twitter!) the Endo Sister community is HUGE on Twitter! Can't believe how many of us there are!

I follow this one lady, she's an Endo Sister (obvs) and she's doing a project for Endometriosis. I will be speaking to her properly when she's got some more time this week! As she tried to get in touch with me last week and I was in hospital.

So she's doing a photography project to raise awareness for Endometriosis. It's not going to be your typical airy fairy Marie Claire photo-shoot... because as we all KNOW... that is NOT Endo! I'm really excited by her project and wanted to get involved.

We had a brief chat and she's left me to have a think about what Endometriosis is to me and to give her a word... yes, just one word! That describes that feeling/emotion/thought whatever. But I have to sum it up in one word. For every woman it is going to mean something different...

Now... where do I start?

FRUSTRATED? – Took so long for a diagnosis, doctors not believing me, being made to feel crazy, not being able to go to work, not being able to socialise properly, not being able to shop.. The list goes on.

RELIEF? – That I KNOW what is wrong with me and I know I can and must fight this. That my family know I'm not crazy, I have a reason for my pain. The

GP's that misdiagnosed me can now see that I was right for all these years.

EMPOWERED? – I want to do more and raise awareness of endo, I want a website, I want every woman to have had the word Endometriosis on their lips, I want to do talks in schools, colleges, uni's, medical schools, I want to raise money and awareness through charity events, I want to start a Charity walk like they do for breast cancer. I want to give back to the Endo community that gave and gave and never stops giving when I need information and support.

LOVED? – By my family, my ever loving boyfriend, my friends, my new friends – all the endosisters who offer their support daily.

It is so, so, so, so difficult to sum up my experience with Endometriosis in just one word.

But I think I have it.

S C A R E D.

Yes. Scared. That is my word.

Scared. Scared because for all those years, I had no idea what the pain was. Scared because I remember how I felt on that one particular morning when I woke up and I couldn't physically move. And I had to shout for my Mum to help my muscles to work and all I could do was cry. Scared because of the amount of blood that was in my bed. Scared because I now finally have a NAME for my condition. Scared because I didn't know what it fully meant and I'm still finding out. Scared that I may never be able to have a child. Scared that I may never be able to have a teenager, a grown adult not just a baby. Scared. Scared that if that is the case that my family and my boyfriend's family will be disappointed.

49

Scared that one day my boyfriend will turn around and say, babe I can't take this anymore, I want children. Even though he says he doesn't care he just wants me to be healthy. Scared of the hospitals. Scared of needles. Scared of every single scan I have to go through. Scared of every internal examination. Scared of gloved hands. Speculums. Swabs. Injections. Medical notes. Scared. Scared. Scared. Scared of the pain, and how intense it can be. Scared of the way it makes me become incredibly angry and so dramatically upset the next. Scared of all the different treatments. How do I know which is the right one for me? Scared of the horror stories. Scared for every single woman out there who has to go through this day in, day out. Scared for all the young girls growing up whose doctors won't listen to them. Scared that the pain may never truly go away and it will constantly be there. Scared that one day I, yes me, I will just give up. Scared.

Yeah, that's my word.
What's yours?

Chapter 13
The Effects of Prostap for Me...

For me, this is going to be quite personal and I know a lot of my friends and family probably won't like reading it. But I need to get it off my chest as I find this really helps me to get things clear in my mind and set things straight. So fingers crossed, this will do that for me! I've touched on things briefly in the past but I've wanted to do this for some time now as I have tried searching Google for the answers to see if anyone has felt the same way I've been feeling but nothing has come up. Just scientific side effects – I know about all of those! I spoke to fellow EndoSisters via Twitter and of course... you all had the answers, some of you felt the same as me when on GnRH Analog. Again, it's quite hard to get in what you want to say in 140 characters... plus like I've said before, I don't want to discuss too much on my twitter. For now, I need to just unload my messy mind so this post will probably be all higgle-de-piggledy and won't make an awful lot of sense but I guess that will just mirror my mentality at the moment!

If you've read previous posts, you will know that I began GnRH Analog injections. In my case, this is otherwise known as Prostap SR. Type this into Google and you always get the same results... side effects, uses, women that have just been brushed off by their doctors/nurses whilst on it. But nowhere can I find HOW to deal with the side-effects.

51

I have been having an injection every 4 weeks; I've had my final one as you know when I've discussed this previously. Thank god. Can't wait for this chemical rubbish to leave my body. As I had adverse side effects to the pill I didn't want to take the daily tablets alongside it. So for me, it was just the injection. I know everybody is different with these injections, some have them 3-monthly etc. I'm not sure of all the different uses and ways of having them so I'm just going to ramble on about my experience for now!

The purpose of having the injections was to help reduce pain, help reduce/shrink the Endo that was there on the surface of my bowel and bladder and to stop my periods for my next surgery. Now, if you HAVE been reading then you will know this is not the case and that my Endo continued to grow, expand, spread... whatever you want to call it!

Hot flushes. Disjointed sleep. No sleep. Emotional. Super insecure. MORE pain. Increased anxiety. Major, major, major depression. No motivation.

At first, I found the hot flushes a problem purely because it was a shock to the system! To have actual droplets of sweat on your body. How the HELL do you get sweaty knees? I didn't think that was even POSSIBLE! I'm just so thankful for the fact I was having these injections over winter! To be waking up constantly with the duvet stuck to my body and my hair smelling of sweat when I woke up in the morning. I'm JUST about getting used to them now I've had my 6th injection, but I find they are lasting longer now which is so strange. The lack of sleep came hand in hand with the hot flushes and increased pain.

That's a point, has anyone else found they have had increased pain? Maybe the fact I've had increased pain is because my Endometriosis has continued to grow causing me to be doubled up in pain. Crying constantly from agony despite being on Oramorph and a cocktail of strong painkillers.

All these I've discovered are pretty much across the board for the majority of women, the hot flushes, lack of sleep etc. What I have been discovering is that not everyone has felt what I'm feeling. Whether that's just because we're all too scared/worried to discuss it. I don't know. I feel I need to. Just in case there is someone else out there right now feeling like I feel and they're on the same treatment. They might read this and realise they're not alone in this.

Full on, hits you in the face, depression.

To the point where I have been so suicidal. I have actually scared myself. At the same time, not given a fuck about what would happen if I was gone. Just being so selfish and not wanting to be in pain anymore.

This Prostap has messed with my head in more ways than one.

I've had thoughts where I could quite easily have gone into the kitchen, got a knife and just cut out my insides. That's how much pain I was in. The knife would not have hurt me because I was already in such intense agony. How could it hurt me?

I know this isn't a nice subject, it's disgusting and depressing but I need to talk about it. Like I said, there might be others out there that have felt like this because of Endometriosis not just because of this silly hormonal treatment.

The amount of times I have told my Mum that I just want to die these past few months is uncountable. I really meant those words. Even now as I'm typing this I can't see a way out of my slump. If it wasn't for my amazing Mum, the most beautiful boyfriend and our gorgeous puppy, keeping me strong, trying to make me happier. I don't think I would still be here.

I know that it IS just the hormonal treatment. In no other event would I EVER consider suicide. But I just haven't been able to help it, when I can't even do a simple thing like get myself a drink from the kitchen because I can't stand because of pain. I don't think it helps that I've been off work because of pain and I've had nothing to get up for really because I can't go anywhere/do anything. I've basically thought to myself, 'what's the point in living?', 'what's the point in being here?', 'if I wasn't here, I wouldn't be in pain anymore', 'why me? I've had enough drama in my life to give Jeremy Kyle another 30 years of episodes, why do I have to have this stupid fucking disease with no cure?'

It has been hard. Very hard.

I didn't want to talk to my boyfriend about it at first, but we can talk to each other about anything and he made me sit down and tell him exactly how I was feeling. He helped me. He helped me so much; I never want to let him go. I think the fact I am going through all this rubbish has made us stronger and brought us even closer together. I've had to keep reminding myself that it IS just the injections; it's the chemicals running riot in my body which are having a negative effect ANYWAY despite the emotional side of things. I tried telling my nurses how it makes me feel but they just go yes, that's a side effect. WHAT? Wanting to slash my own body is a side-effect? Surely that's not normal. But of course, I didn't go into detail. I was ashamed. Embarrassed.

There are times where I feel great. But 80% of the time, I feel like shit. I'm hoping for my period, for the first time in my life. I'm hoping I get my period soon. It will mean Prostap has left my body and I can get my mind back to normal, my life back on track and say FUCK OFF to all these silly insecurities that have cropped up. Paranoia, anxiety, lack of confidence, depression. I can say FUCK OFF to it all.

I feel hopeful now though. I feel like it's becoming clearer in my head and I will get through this. I can't give up. I will keep fighting this AND my surgery will go well and everything will be good for a while.

Anyway, thank you for letting me get that off my chest!

Prostap is a Bitch.

Chapter 14
An average morning for me at the moment...

I wake up, crying because the pain is so intense. I get ready. It takes me hours. Because I have to lie on my bed waiting for painkillers to kick in. When they don't I take my morphine. I wash my face, brush my teeth. Sit down on the bathroom floor because I've become tired. I stand up, I get dizzy, I reach for the glass on the sink, fill it with water. Sit down on the side of the bath and drink. I go into my Make Up room, sit in front of the mirror and don't look at myself because I hate the way I look. I want to take my skin off and throw it away, chop and change my features because I hate the way they are on my face. I open up my moisturiser and apply it to my skin without looking. Just touching, feeling. I lie down on the floor because again, I'm tired.

Waiting for my moisturiser to sink in. I reach for a cotton bud and dip it into my bottle of foundation, and dab onto 5 areas of my face – forehead, nose, cheeks, and chin. Pick up my foundation brush and quickly buff into my skin, it's only now that I look in the mirror, not looking at me... past me. Just making sure every bit of my skin is covered. I feel shy, sick and exhausted. I reach for my eyebrow pencil and start to sketch my eyebrows on, again, not looking in the mirror, just at the eyebrow hairs and making sure the lines are accurate and they look natural but made up at the same time. Perfection. Obsessed. It's only now I look in the mirror properly. I quickly buff in my face powder. I spend a minute or so contouring my face with bronzer and highlighter.

I start to smile. I feel more like me. I apply some of my favourite coral blusher. Sometimes if I can be bothered I line my eyes with my gel eyeliner. This is when I usually feel my best. I have worn eyeliner since I was 12. When I don't wear it, it's because I seriously can't be fucked. Eyeliner makes me feel more confident. I apply two coats of mascara, wiggling the brush from side to side and up the length of my lashes. Top and bottom. I notice my lips are pale. Covered in foundation. I don't look right yet. I sit and choose a lipstick for the day. I usually go for a bright vivid one. The brighter the better. I take a photo. Instagram that shit. Apply a filter. Hashtag the hell out of it. People who know me see my made up face, the fake smile that's slapped on. But they don't look at my eyes, and see what I'm feeling or how long the process takes to make me look normal.

I do this in hospital. I apply my makeup when I'm lying down and can't move. I can be in the MOST horrendous pain, to the point where I am crying. If I start to apply makeup and get creative. It calms me. It takes the focus off my pain.

Once I've finished. I double up in agony again. I change my underwear. I sit on the floor and pull on some leggings. Throw on the nearest top I can reach. Trying to stop myself from crying from the pain. I don't want to smudge my makeup. I need to look good for my boyfriend. This is what I feel. He says I look beautiful without makeup. I don't believe him. Prostap causing me to be insecure. I make my way back to the bed and lie there. Sometimes I cry out in pain, pinching my hand to stop myself from crying. Teddy, our puppy, comes and lies next to me and we wait for my boyfriend to come home from work/training. Now can you, the ones who don't have Endometriosis, understand why I bother to apply my makeup? It gives me a few hours of pain relief. Surely you would do the same if that worked for you. I need to make myself look okay on the outside to feel slightly okay on the inside.

I'm not going to allow people to see me looking at my worst. That is not me. I'm far too insecure for that right now.

Please understand... just because I might look okay... I'm not.

Chapter 15
My Little Visits!

So a couple of weeks ago one of my Besties came to see me to cheer me up as she knew I was in a bad way. She came round with a box of girly heaven for me, and when she was here I couldn't stop crying. It just makes you feel so loved when someone you've known for less than two years cares more about you than someone who's known you for more than ten years. Anyone else get that?

It wasn't even the little gift she'd put so much thought into... it was just seeing her face and getting some cuddles! I love her to bits. She's one of those friends that has been there for me every single step. Even though they have THE busiest, hectic life. She always makes time for me. She's amazing.

And then! This weekend I get a surprise visit from her, one of the girls from work and my manager! Seeing new faces on Sunday was brilliant, and really cheered me up. The fact that again, people had gone out of their way to come and see how I am just made me feel really cared for. My manager had even gone out of her way to find me a Gluten-Free treat... AMAZING. I really, really enjoyed it. And couldn't believe she'd thought of something like that, so special. My other friend from work got me such a cute card which had 'Get well thoughts to brighten your day' which I thought was really cute! Along with a great new book for me to read, 'Sapphire' which is so good because I LOVE reading. And I'm sure I'd told her one day my dream is to have a house with my own personal library in, so for her to get me a book (I mean.. not everybody reads, hard to believe isn't it) was so thoughtful. She also got me a little Angel of Strength which I now keep with me at all times. I particularly need it at the moment!

But again, it's not even that they came with gifts. It was just the fact that they came to see me! Seeing different faces and hearing new gossip and things that were going on at work, having a laugh etc it really helped to cheer me up. Fantastic to see them. Even though I felt incredibly self-conscious the whole time as I hadn't washed my hair in a week, let alone brushed it. I had Teddy's fur all over leggings I'd worn 4 days straight. Putting it bluntly I looked like an absolute tramp. And I had twitches from the amount of medication I'm on but luckily I don't think they noticed. Bloody hope not anyway. Oh and the house was a mess. I'm very house proud but I just haven't got the energy lately to tidy up/clean put things away. I know it sounds disgusting but jeez... It takes me an average of four hours to get out of bed. How the hell am I going to clean? Have to thank my Mum and my boyfriend's Mum and Nana for that for helping out whenever they come up. Genuinely appreciate it. Just wish I wasn't ill because there's no way in hell I'd allow others to clean my house for me if I had the energy and strength. Too independent it's kind of difficult letting go of things at the minute. Feel so dependent on everyone else and I can't stand it.

So yes, that's a summary of my recent little visits that have helped to keep me going.

I don't really have much to talk about to be honest. Aside from an overnight visit at the hospital and being in ever increasing pain. Luckily, I'm back at the hospital next week for my Sigmoidoscopy. Which I will be writing about in full detail. As yet again, I can't find ANY information about this anywhere and I'm pretty nervous. As people told me the Barium Enema wouldn't hurt. Well it pissed off my Endo and caused it to flare up and I've been in daily pain ever since and it just won't go. So yeah, you could say I'm more than nervous. I don't want the Sigmoidoscopy to irritate my Endo but at the same time I know that it is vital for my surgery and I'm just going to have to get on with it. No choice.

I can't get rid of this pain and painkillers aren't helping. I tried some increased painkillers but they made me feel incredibly weird, spaced out and just seeing things. So I came off those. Worked for the pain, but couldn't hack the side effects. So I don't really have all that much to tell you. I don't want to bore you moaning about my pain. I want to provide you with interesting, funny things... which is pretty hard to do at the minute. I'm used to being the life and soul of everything and the fact I can't even do simple tasks like wash up without getting incredibly tired at the moment is so so so depressing.

Ups and downs...

Chapter 16
Flexible Sigmoidoscopy and the Drink of Doom

Yes… as the title suggests this post is about the Flexible Sigmoidoscopy scan I had done the other day. Some of you will be asking, 'What the hell is that?' Some will be wondering, 'What happens, I have to have one soon?' Others will be reading this, 'Oh yes... I remember having one, the prep medication was much worse than the procedure!' Obviously, so far I have wrote about everything in as much detail as possible, and have tried to be as honest as I can be; that's what I'm going to try and do today.

This is my experience with what happened and yes... I was a big, big, big baby!

So the night before, I set about filling in the medical forms. Just basic questionnaires, which medication am I on etc. Very boring. I also had to take two tablets which help to kick start bowel movements. I've taken these in the past they're known as Dulcolax. Or it's proper term 'Bisacodyl 5mg'.

Easiest part!

Then I begin a very restless nights sleep. I was so stressed and nervous about what was to happen the next day. I woke on the hour every hour till I had to be awake and up at 6am to begin drinking the Drink of Doom.

Before I go on, I want to have a little rant. It's the 21st century, surely they've invented something we don't have to drink and we can just take a tablet washed down with a litre of water? Blah.

The Drink of Doom is really called MoviPrep. I received two sachets. One was a smallish sachet labelled SACHET B and the other was an A5 sized sachet labelled SACHET A. I then had to mix these both together in a jug filled with a litre of water. I had to empty Sachet A in parts as it sat on top of the water and wasn't going in so I had to stir and then add more. I felt like I was baking. I then had to fill a glass with half a litre of water. The Drink of Doom I had created was to be drunk over a 2 hour period... so by 8.30 I was to have finished drinking.

First glass...

It's pretty cloudy looking! I took my first gulp... tasted like lemon. Tasted like the exact same thing I had to drink in hospital that caused severe pain, being sick and passing out. I instantly got it into my head that I was going to get really ill from this, and I just didn't want to do it. It was that TASTE. You know when you've had something to eat in the past, something bad happened and you can never eat it again? Or you can't stand to smell a certain thing because it just reminds me you of something else? That's what I had at 6.30am after hardly any sleep, very cranky mood and in excruciating pain.

I keep trying. I'm now crying, breathing heavy and really trying to force this drink down my neck. I'm the kind of girl that used to be able to down pints in the pub as dares... I don't have a problem drinking vile drinks! But this... I think it was the fact that I'd had a bad experience with a previous one so I just had it in my head that it was going to cause that insane amount of pain again, and I was scared. I was tweeting like mad on Twitter that I couldn't do it, and everyone who messaged me back was being supportive, and that helped me to finish the first glass by 8am. An hour and a half to drink 250ml... I had another 750ml to go! What was I going to do? I'd rang my mum at 7.30am and told her I couldn't do it. I sat in the bathroom, kneeling on the toilet and was screaming and I couldn't breathe and then I was on the edge of a panic attack. I had worked myself up that much. This stuff had started to taste like chlorine by this point. I'd convinced myself I was going to be poisoned by it and I just didn't want to be in the pain I'd had to go through in hospital where I'd passed out on the floor after vomiting everywhere and I'd had those excruciating pains. I was SCARED. Mum was still on the phone, calming me down telling me I had to do it – just hearing her voice got me through another half glass. My Mum used to be a nurse so I think that helps, I needed her.

I think I said something on Twitter like, I feel like Dumbledore when he had to drink that drink from the goblet in Tom Riddle/Voldermort's cave... but at least he had Harry to help him! Because I'd been crying so much my boyfriend woke up and he then tried helping me drink it, by this point though... I'd had enough. I was screaming and then decided point blank that I wasn't drinking anymore and that was it. He said I had to drink it, so I picked up my glass and jug and went back in the bathroom and locked myself in and was crying and screaming and then I decided that I couldn't care less about doing this scan for the operation. I'm sick of all these bullshit tests and crap, I just want my surgery, I want a fucking cure. At this point my boyfriend had somehow got the bathroom door unlocked and got me back to bed and calmed me down and tried getting me to drink it again. I drank some more and then just refused as it was now making me gag.

It all seems silly now I'm writing about what happened, it is just a drink after all. But hey, I'm being honest.

As my boyfriend was downstairs fixing me a hot water bottle it was 8.30am and I'd been on the phone to Mum again, who was now stuck in traffic as she'd rushed out to come to our house. And I was like Mum, I'm not drinking anymore, I refuse, do I have to drink it all? I've drank half, I can't do anymore. Mum was telling me that I HAD to drink it, I told her I've done half and the 2 hours are up now anyway, so what can I do? I then don't remember anything else apart from falling asleep with my boyfriend's arms around me after hearing my Mum say I didn't have to drink anymore.

The next minute my Mum was in our room (my boyfriend had clearly let her in), and she was making me show her what I'd drank and then she started getting my things together and got me some morphine as I was in so much pain. I then staggered to the toilet... nothing. Just air. Mum was taking me back to her house, so I could sleep and use the toilet and then go straight to the hospital as it's only round the corner. Mum started gathering up my things I would need with my boyfriend's help whilst I just cried a lot because I was freaking out about the scan. I wanted to get to Mum's house so badly but I was so scared that I would just end up going to the toilet in the car! Mum looked at me and said don't be ridiculous, I'm a nurse, I've seen it all before, if it happens, it happens! We have towels!

So I get in the car, and instantly light up a cigarette. So that quitting smoking lasted well didn't it? I was so stressed out, I had severe cramping in my belly – I couldn't determine if it was Endo pain or the Drink of Doom. It's about a 25 minute drive to my Mum's home. We get there and I go to the toilet and it was like someone had switched a tap on. For the next few hours I was on the toilet and off the toilet, looking in the mirror to see if my bloated Endo belly had gone down. It's been months since I've seen it flat and toned, I've been constantly bloated for the past few months. Depressing. I was in and out of Mum's amazing huge, comfy bed. I didn't want to leave her bed, it was like a cosy nest and I felt so safe from the world and from my Endometriosis.

It's now nearing 12pm, we have to leave at half 12 so I start getting ready. I used a face wipe on my skin. Which if anyone knows me (I work in skincare) will KNOW that this is something I absolutely just do not, ever DO. It ruins your skin. But I seriously could NOT be bothered. I had no moisturiser with me, I had to use Mum's but she uses the same brand as me (the one I work for) so I was happy even though it wasn't one for my particular skin type! I even couldn't be bothered doing my makeup... erm, hello? Again, this is not me! When I say this... I don't mean any at all... I just mean I had face powder but no liquid foundation, no bronzer just blush, no contour. I basically had... face powder, blusher, eyebrows and mascara and a swipe of lipstick... This is MINIMAL for me. Seriously. I needed SOME on... my war face!

I wore my new tracksuit pants which my boyfriend bought for me just so I would be comfy on the day. They're purple colour too, which is my favourite! I was so grateful for these as my belly was just in spasm and because they were new it made the journey to hospital a bit better and I felt like my boyfriend was with me (he couldn't be, as he had work) which I know sounds silly as they're only pants.. But it did!!

I arrive with Mum and get to the right unit, and we enter reception and I hand my details in to the receptionist. On the walls are photos of what happens during a sigmoidoscopy which were actually quite calming. It took you through the process of what happens when you arrive, right through to when you leave. I only had to wait a short time until my name was called along with three other women; this was where I had to leave my Mum. She had to wait in the main reception and couldn't come any further. At this point, I just wanted to cry and started freaking out; Mum said she'll text me. Off I go with the nurse and the three other women who were there for their different scans. We are taken down a long corridor and on the way I start talking to the other ladies and say, I hope I'm not the only one who is petrified? We all have a chat about how scared we are and how awful the medication prep drink / Drink of Doom was. We are then taken to a little waiting room and told to sit down until our names are called. After a few minutes I was the only one left. I was left waiting for around 10 minutes but in this time because I was alone, I was freaking out and I was being an absolute baby, but it's purely because I didn't REALLY know what to expect! I was so terrified that the scan would affect and piss off my Endometriosis and cause bitter pain again.

My name is called and I am then introduced to the nurse that will be looking after me, she was incredibly warm and lovely. I am steered towards a comfy chair within a cute little cubicle type area with another chair opposite. Here is where I have to sign documentation and she goes through things like, 'Could I be pregnant'... no, I'm menopausal so I highly doubt it. I am then taken to my own bed where she has laid out two hospital gowns, a pair of blue shorts in a plastic bag, a plastic bag to put my belongings in. I am to put a hospital gown on the front and one on the back so I am covered. The blue shorts have a 'bum flap' which make me laugh.

I then spend some time just sitting on the chair whilst I wait for my nurse to come back and do my blood pressure and sedation which I have asked for just to help relax me as I was so scared.

She comes back in and applies the cannula ready for the sedation to go in when I'm in the surgery room or whatever you want to call it! My surgeon's assistant comes in – well, I think she was an assistant, she did introduce herself. I don't know whether she was learning or what, I have no idea, can't remember! She was lovely and straight to the point anyway. I had to sign some MORE documents and then she disappeared and then ANOTHER nurse came to get me, and asked me to put my Converse back on to walk to the room. I told her I was petrified. This nurse was so so sweet, a cute little voice and everything, she's in the right job anyway!

I enter the room; it's got a few student doctors in there and the nurses. I was so scared, I really wasn't bothered. I'm told to lie on the bed and my surgeon says hello and then I'm shown how to use the Gas and Air and then some sedation goes in through the cannula. They do a finger insertion first just to check everything and then in he goes with the camera. I didn't feel it go in, and didn't particularly feel much throughout the procedure, although I did puff on the gas and air numerous times at particularly wincey parts. It was great as I could see on the screen what was happening and the nurses were speaking to me the whole time. I was having great fun because I felt so high on the gas and air and they were making me laugh, or I was making them laugh, I'm not sure!

He spoke to me and told me how far up he was, according to every single scan I've had so far (from the MRI to the Barium Enema) they all indicate that the Endometriosis has pushed through the bowel wall and caused narrowing on my bowel passage at around 14cm up to 17cm. He got all the way to around 24cm? I think from what I remember and everything was absolutely clear! Something must have been shining down on me... how can scans indicate it's gone through the bowel wall and then I have this done.. And it hasn't?! I feel so incredibly lucky. That the Endo is just on the outside which has caused some narrowing because it's pressing down, but so far nothing has gone through. During the procedure he did have to give me a wash / enema as I hadn't drank all the MoviPrep not everything was completely clear (I didn't tell anyone that I hadn't drank it) but as soon as he said he couldn't find any sign of

Endometriosis or adhesion's I just started crying from relief. To know that it's just on the outside! So happy! Afterwards he explained that the surgery is already scheduled in for himself and my gynaecologist surgeon to operate in May. I haven't got the exact date yet but to know that's it's oh so close is fantastic news.

I am then wheeled back out to the recovery rooms where I have my blood pressure checked and it was like 96 or something, they wouldn't let me go till it was a 100. I was given a lot of biscuits and some juice! Yummy custard cream biscuits! The best. I then decide I want to get changed but I'm worried at this point that I have leaked everywhere but I had a pad on the bed so it was ok.

When my blood pressure was above a 100, I was good to go and I just had to go into yet another room and the nurse explained everything I'd had done and I was given a piece of paper with everything on it and then she walked me back through to meet my Mum in the main reception area. Where I started crying to my Mum as I told her the Endo hadn't gone through the bowel wall! She was so happy and helped me walk back to the car and we drove back to her house and I got back in bed and rested. I was in a bit of pain after, I think it was due to the fact the medication was still working and I was still going to the toilet!

When I got to mums I just ended up getting cosy in her bed and drinking peppermint tea which helps relieve the trapped air they blow into your bowel. Relaxing before getting back in the car and heading home, where my Mum helped me out and fixed me a hot water bottle and got me my pain killers and made me some food to eat.

So yeah, that's pretty much the ins and outs of my experience with a Flexible Sigmoidoscopy. My Mum and my boyfriend were absolutely incredible on this day, and both were there for me when I truly needed them. I was so so exhausted and I actually had a decent nights sleep. But the next day I was in an intense amount of pain and was struggling to move.

Just want to say my Mum is the best, I couldn't ask for anyone better to have been there throughout. For every single appointment, every hospital phone call, every injection, every scan, and every procedure. She's my world.

Some tips >>>
Down each gulp of the Drink of Doom with apple juice or flat lemonade... I had neither in the house. Lesson learnt.

Have a friend or family member present to help you drink the drink... that's if you're anything like me anyway

Peppermint Tea for afterwards

Sanitary Towel just to be on the safe side... trust me!

The majority of you will probably be way braver than me... but I'm not usually a baby but I just found this incredibly difficult. Please try not to judge me or laugh at me... I'm just being honest.

I just want to say that every single member of staff at the unit were outstanding, and so caring, gentle and funny... I hope all the unit's around the world are like this one as it really helped make the experience easier.

Chapter 17
Hot Flushing Hell. And the F word < Don't read if offended by swearing.

I need to vent. I finished my Prostap injections last month... like nearly 6 weeks ago now. I'm so upset. I'm STILL having hot flushes? WHY? How long does this happen for? Why am I still having side effects? Why am I still feeling so fucking suicidal? I'm sorry for my language! I feel like SHIT. I'm looking in the mirror and thinking WHO ARE YOU? I have no idea who the hell I am today.

Do you ever have these days? Where you have no idea who you are and what the hell it is you're supposed to be doing in life?

I'm lay in bed, having a super long hot flush... It's been going on now for a good 30 minutes. Seriously? What is with that? Oh and I've forgotten to mention that every time I get a hot flush, it kick starts another big wave of pain. I'm trying to soldier this out right now but I can't do it by myself.

My boyfriend is at the stadium as there's a game today and he won't be home until after 9ish. My mum is at work too and my besties are all in work. So all I have at this moment in time is this writing to vent out the whirlwind that is going on in my head.

AARGHHHHHHHH.

And now the other thing going through my head is... what if I never start my periods again?

I want my chance to try for a baby. Where's my goddamn fucking period?

Why did I agree to this forced chemical menopause? Oh that's right it was supposed to SHRINK my Endometriosis. Well guess what... it fucking hasn't. It's caused it to spread and expand like a mother fucking sumo wrestler eating cake. Someone please explain why we are made to go through this old fashioned bullshit idea that going through the menopause works for Endometriosis? I want to hear from the women who it's worked for and I want to hear from the women it hasn't worked for. How, how, how, HOW can it work when we all KNOW that even when you've had a hysterectomy you can still suffer with Endometriosis.. So pray tell me why the fuck they still insist that hormonal treatment like this will work. To me, now I've been through it, it's like the stupid bullshit crap that comes out of people's mouths that having a baby gets rid of Endo because you have no periods during that time...FUCK! NO IT DOESN'T. We all know that. Periods are only a SMALL part of Endo. Those that have Endometriosis know this all too well.

Oh and to the nurse months ago that said, 'Having a baby will help with your Endometriosis'... please explain to me how you came to that conclusion? When... I'm going through the forced chemical menopause and my Endo has continued to grow/expand whatever. What makes you so SURE that if I were by some miracle to get pregnant... would it HELP my Endo? Surely just like being on the menopause, the Endo will still be there, and still grow and get bigger and continue to create massive concave holes in my path to my dreams. Every time I walk down the path, Endo strikes like a bitter poisonous snake, so fast I didn't see it coming, and I drop into the cavernous hole in the ground and I have to dig myself out of it once more to get back on the path.

Right now, I feel like staying in the hole and filling it in forever.

Help.

Chapter 18
My latest visit to hospital :)

I hope everyone is feeling good and if you're not... I'm thinking of you and I hope you have the support around you like I have.

I'm actually struggling to write this as right now I'm so zombie-fied it's untrue! I've had a little trip to hospital and had my pain meds changed. It all started last week. My mum and boyfriend wanted me to go to hospital but I said no, I'll see how I get on. Me, being stubborn trying to soldier it out, hoping the pain would just... leave. Uh uh. It didn't. The day after they were saying I should go, my boyfriend was in work as was my Mum and I had no-one to call. I was getting worse and worse as the day went on and I'd been sick a few times from the pain of it all; couldn't stop screaming in agony and then my Manager rang me. Obviously when you see your manager calling, I shut up and answered the phone. She knew something was wrong and I kept saying I'm okay and she told me I had to ring my boyfriend to take me to hospital. So after a chat, that's what I did. If it hadn't been for my manager, I wouldn't have rang my boyfriend. I didn't want to get him out of work or worry him. So, I just want to say thanks to her... she's been so supportive over the past few months.

As soon as my boyfriend answered that was it... just hearing his voice made me start crying! I was so stressed out that it had made my pain worse. He told me to calm down as I was having a panic attack because I was so scared. I mean why is my pain increasing daily? It is scary. I can't handle it anymore truth be told. Within 15 minutes he was walking through the door and picking up my Endo hospital bag (just in case I was admitted) that he had bought especially for occasions like these and was fixing me some Oramorph and a hot water bottle and getting me in the car.

The car journey was awful... every red light! Why, why, why in these situations does this happen? We get to hospital and manage to find a car parking slot straight away. My boyfriend helps me to the A&E department and I register at the front desk, and tell them what the situation is. I take a seat with my boyfriend and wait for the Triage nurse. After around 20 minutes or so... if that to be honest, the Triage nurse called my name and I went through into the room with my boyfriend. I had my hot water bottle with me still for comfort and heat (more on that later, grr). I explained to her that I have Endometriosis and I'm awaiting dual surgery with two consultants as it is on my bowel and other places. She asks me what medication I've had, so I tell her... the Tramadol, Naproxen, Paracetamol and Oramorph which I had taken more than I was allowed to at home with the Oramorph. She asked me when the pain started and I told her last week, and that each day was getting worse and worse and today I just couldn't hack it. I had been sick a few times from the pain. She asks what my pain scales is on a 1-10, I say is there higher than 10? She looks at me a bit funny and I say... I know most people would be screaming and crying but I'm in so much pain I'm out of energy for those dramatics. She tells me to wait where I am with my boyfriend and she goes out the other door on the other side. There is one door (well curtain) leading out into A&E waiting room and then a door on the opposite side leading out into the bay where ambulance patients arrive.

She comes back around 10 minutes or so later and said right follow me. So we did! She leads me to one of the beds in the A&E department (there are 17 in total), I was bed 16. I'm thinking eh? This is different. As usually, I get sent for a pointless blood test and pointless swabs and told to wait back in the main waiting area. The Triage nurse informs me she's sending someone to take my blood and getting someone to administer more painkillers. She also tells us that she has sent for a Obs & Gynae doctor to come down and assess me and that I will be being admitted onto Jasmine Suite to get my pain under control.

A nurse comes in and puts a cannula into the crease of my elbow and she recognises me, so we're having a chat about that, just how I'm getting on and stuff. She then begins to take some blood which I joke about how it looks like Ribena or Vimto. Then some Doctor in charge on the A&E department comes to speak to me... tells me off about my hot water bottle and starts prodding my belly. Erm, excuse me... you prodding my belly for? Read my NOTES. And then goes on and on about the hot water bottle again and how it will cause blisters – WHO CARES? I'M IN PAIN. He then says I'm not allowed it anymore and empties it down the sink. Yeah... I didn't like him. He then says someone will be over with some painkillers.

So I'm sat there thinking, great… what's it going to be, bloody codeine or something? I have that at home! A nurse comes in and starts putting morphine into my cannula…bit by bit. I've never had it intravenously before and wow... that is enough to get you hooked! You feel this huge wave come over you and you feel as if your body is shutting down. She asked me what my pain was I said a 7... She said right… she put some more in, she asked me again… a 4… she put some more in… I was pain free, dizzy, and disorientated but pain free. She says right you've had the full lot there, I said can I go home now then, now you've sorted my pain? She laughed and said no... You can't have this all the time so we need to figure something else out for you. She was a funny nurse, I liked her.

My Mum then turned up just as I'd had all this morphine so my boyfriend was filling her in on what had happened as at this point I was feeling pretty weird. The Obs & Gynae Doctor then arrived to see me and she recognised me straight away but couldn't place my name. I said I sold a certain skincare brand and she said Oh yes! You sold it to me one time, I remember now! She had also been to see me the last time I was in hospital! So we had a chat, and she said right you're going onto Jasmine Suite and we're going to arrange for Pain Management to come and see you in the morning.

So I get taken up to Jasmine Suite where there is a bed ready and waiting. By this time the morphine they had given me in A&E had begun to wear off so I asked if it was possible to have some more painkillers. I was told yes. This was half 11 at night. HALF TWO IN THE MORNING… I'M STILL WAITING. By this point I'm incredibly stressed out as I didn't want to harass the nurse that was on the night shift as she'd already been in and taken my meds off me for control or whatever. I said the ones in the tablet case are higgledy piggledy as I've not organised them yet and she said, 'Well, how are you supposed to know what to take' or something along those lines, and said it really abruptly and rudely. So I felt like I couldn't ask for more painkillers. And then it got too much, half 2 in the morning... I ring my buzzer which took me 15 minutes to get hold of as I was in agony, couldn't move and they hadn't even put it close to my bed, so I really struggled getting that. Then... they bring me ORAMORPH. The f'in point? At this point I was wishing I was at home... at least at home I could have as much Oramorph as I wanted and when I wanted. I was so incredibly stressed out it was making my pain worse. As I'm sure a lot of you know what stress can do to you!

I couldn't sleep. I think I fell asleep at around half 5 and was awake again by 7 begging to have some more medication. Meds didn't come round till 8am. All I wanted to do was go in the bathroom and hurt myself. Just to take away the pain. I seriously didn't want to be on this planet. One of the worst nights of my life. The pain was so torturous... I still can't understand why my body wants to hurt me this way.

I spent another night in hospital. I won't talk about everything but I will say that after I'd seen Pain Management, my prescription was sent off to the Pharmacy and I had another pain attack because at this point, Tramadol had been crossed off my prescription and replaced with the MST – Slow release morphine. All

I was left with was Paracetamol... I'd had those an hour before. I was literally trying not to scream as I didn't want to disturb anyone else on the ward so I got my legs up to my chest as high as they would go and curled up in a ball, rocking gently and crying, trying to contain my screams and breathing deeply. Writhing around like a woman possessed. The lady in the bed diagonally opposite me pressed the buzzer for a nurse and they came and couldn't stop saying sorry to me as they couldn't give me anything not even the Oramorph whilst my prescription was in Pharmacy. There is one amazing nurse there, who was rubbing my back and saying nice things to help calm me down. She is fantastic. Don't know what that ward would do without her. My Oramorph had been doubled in dosage as well... which was the frustrating thing.

Long story short, I ask to go home on my new painkillers and my boyfriend comes to collect me and we live happily ever after. Haha joking. I need a nap.

Do Fairytales come true?

Chapter 19
Tired... So tired, even my tired is tired.

Well, I was supposed to be updating and continuing where I left off previously and letting you know what happened at the hospital. I will… just right now, I'm so tired. I'm more than exhausted. I'm tired of being at home constantly. I want to be back at work but I can't because of the stupid morphine that makes me so sleepy and high. I wouldn't care; it doesn't even do much for my pain. Don't get me wrong, it reduces it dramatically, I truly doubt that anything will make me pain free until my surgery. So I'm just going to have to keep biting my bottom lip, hold back my tears and crack on.

What I will talk about is what I've been doing to distract myself from the pain. I have been baking cupcakes… albeit not very well! I'm learning and I attempted my first butter cream frosting today... hasn't turned out too badly either. My boyfriend went out and bought me a heap of decorating materials. He's the best! He's doing everything he can to keep me entertained whilst I'm stuck at home doing nada. I've never been the type to just sit around doing nothing. I always need to be doing SOMETHING.

I have missed out on so many holidays this year... it's actually depressing. I wanted to go to Amsterdam, Berlin and Copenhagen. This year was the year I was going to travel around Europe using the alphabet. Uh uh. Endo has got in the damn way. Constantly shutting me down this year. Oh and I forgot to mention this weekend I was supposed to go to Northern Ireland for the motorbike racing, North West 200's. Gutted doesn't even begin to describe how I feel about that.

I have a date for my surgery. June 20th... That's the main piece of information from my hospital trip... that's something the hospital trip achieved anyway. My gynae has blocked out the whole entire day for me, so I'm hoping that it doesn't change and that my other surgeon is STILL available for that day too. Now I'm just counting down the days. Can't wait for it to arrive. I just want it done with. I want to get out of the damn house.

I'm sorry this is so wishy washy.

Nap time.

Chapter 20
Bleeding Hell and a Pre-Op

I've been so tired all I wanted to do was lie down in bed and do nothing. I have all these things I need to get done and I just haven't had the energy. Anyway, enough of that; I have some great news!

So if you remember I was stressing about the fact that I haven't had a period since stopping the dreaded Prostap injections (otherwise known as a GNrH Analog injection)! Well... IT HAPPENED! Yes... I woke up on the 6th June with even more excruciating pain than usual... got up, went to the toilet and BOOM! It was pretty disgusting. Wasn't a normal period. All brown and black. At first I was so incredibly happy that it had happened, as it means things are working for me. As the days went on I just wanted it gone. I'm sure the ones that have been through the chemically induced menopause understand that feeling!

For the couple of weeks leading up to that day, I kept saying to my boyfriend that I felt like I was coming on a period and every time I went to the toilet and there was nothing there, I was getting more and more frustrated; Until I just put my extra pain down to Endo and not period cramping.

I should have known, I was kicking off about the fact there was no chocolate in the house! Every day I would ask my boyfriend to get me a bar of chocolate. We had biscuits... NO. I needed BARS of the good stuff.

When I crave chocolate, I'm seriously like a heroin addict needing their next fix. I'm majorly cranky, snappy and can only fixate on getting my chocolate hit! The day I told my boyfriend that I started my period and I was crying and just generally being me on a period; overly emotional etc. He came home with 8 bars of chocolate, a bag of chocolate chip cookies (the big chewy ones, mmm!) and also brought home some chicken wings for me to eat there and then as he knows I crave those too! To top it off, he brought home a magazine for me to read as well!

When he walked in with all those, I just burst into tears and couldn't stop crying. I think I freaked him out, but I couldn't help it. All week I'd been going absolutely MENTAL! Just going on about needing chocolate and screaming in pain, not being able to move, couldn't even do the washing up. Oh, I was a nightmare. And that just made me cry! I love him so much, he's absolutely incredible. I mean EIGHT BARS OF CHOCOLATE – my favourites too! Milka Happy Cow and Cadbury's Dairy Oreo! Oh my life. Incredible.

Oh wowwww!

My period lasted for 7 days and I ran out of chocolate on the 4th day. Not bad going!

So that happened!

Last Friday (14th June) I had to be at the hospital for my pre-op at 11.30am. For those that have never had a pre-op... it's basically an assessment of your general health and writing up what medication you're on, that kind of thing. So I was asked a heap of questions about my health, have I been ill lately aside from my condition etc. Then I had my lungs tested, my heart checked, my pulse taken. Then I had my bloods taken. It's a very quick process... that they DRAG OUT. I left at 1... RIDICULOUS. Seriously... I don't actually understand why one person can't do everything. I was seen by THREE different types of people. One to take my blood, another to take my pulse and have a look in my mouth and listen to my breathing and another to ask me a load of questions. My Mum couldn't understand why they're not trained to do everything. She is trained to do everything! She found it odd. Anyway that's beside the point, the main thing that happened was I was finally handed my letter for my surgery (SHOULD HAVE BEEN IN THE POST AGES AGO) and a prescription for Fleet (To this day I still can't believe I have to pay for pre-meds, stupid thing) and on the prescription it also said..

LOW RESIDUE DIET TO BE FOLLOWED FOR 5 DAYS

My first question to the woman who was asking me every question under the sun was "What is a Low Residue Diet?"

She said it would be written on my prescription sheet. She didn't know. She didn't say she didn't know but she was so brief and blasé about it. I kept asking. I then asked the lady who was checking my chest and things. She didn't know either. Both of their responses were, it will be on the sheet they give you in pharmacy.

Surely, a pre-op team would know the answer to this question? RIDICULOUS.

I then Google it but I clearly read a wrong website as it said it's a diet of white bread and milk. I can't eat either of those things. Cue me stressing and having a rant as we walked down the corridor towards the pharmacy to get my prescription.

I ask at the pharmacist and THEY didn't know. They try printing me a sheet off the system with a diet plan on it. It wouldn't work. Their response was to get in touch with my Surgeon's secretary. I just thought I'll figure it out myself.

And thank you so so so so much to all my EndoDolls on Twitter. You are all so incredibly helpful. To all the beautiful women who sent me photos of their information sheets for the diet, I thank you!

It is now Monday and my surgery is on Thursday, so I don't have to be on this diet for that much longer. It's so hard, I love eating and the fact I'm having to have food restricted well it makes me cranky!

Ohhh, I feel so much better since I've had a rant! Thank you for reading!

Let the countdown continue…

Chapter 21
Discussion Day!

So yesterday was FINALLY the day I got to speak to my amazing surgeon about the surgery that I will be having this Thursday. As most of my Twitter Endo Dolls know, I have been majorly stressing about this as I'm the type of girl that wants to know everything – like every minute little detail! Some people aren't like that, the less they know the better. But I am a control freak and need to know absolutely everything I possibly can!

It was so good to see him; he makes you feel so calm, secure and safe. He's always so smiley too! I wish all Endo Dolls could be treated by him as he's incredible.

The long and short of it is that basically they won't know until they get in there and see everything EXACTLY what has to be done. But we have a rough idea. I will be having the Endometriosis on my bowel shaved off. If it weakens the bowel wall then I will be having a ton of stitches there. Although I am lucky that the Endo hasn't gone right through the wall it has caused a big indentation – this is the bit that won't become clear until during surgery. My water pipe will be released as it's stuck; my left ovary also appears to be stuck so again that will be released. Hopefully all the Endometriosis will be gone on the left from the previous lap. And then he will be excising Endometriosis from the right side. I have been having a ton of pain on the right which I have never really experienced before, so we shall find out tomorrow what the lowdown is there.

I don't really want to talk too much about what is going on – as it makes it all real somehow, you know! All I can tell you is 1/100 chance of a colostomy bag... usually it's a 1/400 chance. But a lot of Endo Dolls have reassured me about this. So I can only hope and pray for a great outcome.

So currently, I'm staying with my Mum at her house. I came straight from hospital yesterday as the prep you have to have always causes me pain but so far I'm doing ok. The drink was nowhere near as bad as what you have to have for a sigmoidoscopy – as it's only a little glass so I can handle it. Although before I drank it, I did have a mini breakdown. Surgery preps are alright to be honest. I'm just trying to remember to drink lots of water! I drank it at 11 and it's now half 2 and so far... NADA. Ah well… I'm sure it will happen soon!

I'm missing my beautiful puppy, Teddy and my amazing boyfriend so much. My boyfriend rang me this morning and told me Teddy didn't sleep well last night (he normally sleeps right through) and he was crying this morning. Just Face Timed my best friend who is looking after Teds today and he was crying in the background which made me sad! She's currently on Face Time to me right now and putting his harness on him to take him on a walk! Can't wait to see him later! I Face Timed my boyfriend yesterday and he put the iPad on the ground right near him but propped up. I called Teddy and he looked at the screen all confused with his head cocked to one side and then came running to the screen and licked it! Last time I came out of hospital he was so excited and sat on my lap licking my face for half an hour! I can't wait to see my boyfriend either.

I am petrified for tomorrow. I am sorry it's not that informative right now. I will be as detailed as possible after my surgery.

One day to go...

Chapter 22
My Second Surgery... Part One!

I think last time, I was talking about how scared I was. Well... I did it! I got through it. Again, thank you so much to everyone who wished me luck and was thinking of me as it really helped me! I've pretty much decided this will be a sort of walk-through of the day... and bits and pieces I remember; please don't expect much as it's all quite vague!

So I managed to drink another one of those drinks, you had to leave a 4-6 hour gap in between the drinks. Nothing like that horrible Drink of Doom though!

The night before my surgery, I was heavily freaking out and couldn't sleep properly and I had to keep reminding myself how incredibly skilled my surgeon is and also my other surgeon who was to be operating on the day. Mum said to me, imagine how you would feel if you were at the other hospital (it's basically condemned... you go in and don't come out). Then she said oh, actually you wouldn't even be treated there, I would have you moved. So she made me laugh about that. I think I was tweeting a lot the evening before and obsessing a lot with Candy Crush and getting mad because I'm stuck on level 135 – it's so frustrating!

I felt a lot calmer after I'd been on Face Time to my boyfriend and our puppy, it was hard being away from them but it was so great being at my Mum's. I really hope everyone has an amazing support network like I have. No-one should have to go through this drama without someone being there for them whether it's by their side or just knowing someone is thinking of you and hoping you're ok.

I wake up in the morning at around 7? Which was quite early and I tried to go back to sleep for a bit. Then at 8 I got up and ran myself a bath as I'd decided the evening before with the help of the Endo Dolls on twitter that it would help relax me in the morning. Oh boy, am I so glad I took their advice! I'd been stressing out so much it had caused the world's biggest pain flare.

The moment my back touched that warm, heavenly soothing water, I just felt every inch of my body relax. As you're probably aware by now, I use makeup application as pain relief these days. So the fact I'd chosen to wash and curl my hair on the day really helped me seen as though you are not allowed to wear makeup on the day of surgery! I got out of the bath, wrapped a towel on my head, sat down in front of the mirror, towel dried my hair and wrapped it back up in the towel on top of my head. I then applied my AMAZING Kiehl's Ultra Facial Cream moisturiser, this stuff is incredible. It's pure 24 hour hydration. I thought, I need this... I need to look good when I wake up! Thank god I did, my skin felt so soft and had a healthy glow to it! I then began to dry and curl my hair. After I did this, I had to break the rules slightly and put my eyebrow make up on.. There was no way I was leaving the house without those bad boys sketched on! As soon as I had done this, I felt much better.

Then I remembered that I still hadn't finished packing my bag for hospital yet. Always last minute! It's the best way. I thought I would just give a quick breakdown of the amount of stuff I take with me that I don't even need or use. There is honestly no need for all this stuff, well, I needed it. I treat the hospital as a holiday, it's the only way I get through it without going insane.

I had my special Endo bag to take with me, it says on it 'I fight like a girl'.. Hell yeah, I do! That's the bag my boyfriend bought for me, if anyone remembers that from a previous post! Packed inside I had:

The post-surgery lilac tracksuit pants that my boyfriend bought me which I wore to my sigmoidoscopy

A variety of different vest tops – all white.. I just have a thing about white tees in hospital!

Pyjama bottoms – two pairs of polka dot ones – love a bit of polka dot

Some shorts (they look hot with the hospital stockings haha – you have to stay looking good right?)

Fresh underwear – I took way more than what I needed but hey, I wasn't sure how long I would be staying!

My amazing customised Barbie hairbrush

Make Up – Foundation, Brows, Gel eyeliner, Selection of eyeshadows, 6 Different lipsticks, Mascara, Face powder, Bronzer, Blusher, Concealer

Make Up brushes – freshly cleaned

Kiehl's Lip Balm

Socks – couple of pairs of normal, never matching and a pair of fluffy socks for comfort

Sanitary Towels – Always pack these.. hospital one's are awful

Some mini packs of cereal

Peppermint Teabags

Magazines

Books pre-downloaded onto iPhone

Dressing Gown – my fave Ted Baker one which is a thin one, I always get too hot in hospital, and it was purely for going down to surgery in

Hair bobble and a few hair grips

Toothbrush, mouthwash

Baby wipes

Kiehl's Ultra Facial Oil-Free Cleanser, Blue Herbal Gel
Spot Treatment (just in case I got a breakout) and
Kiehl's Ultra Facial Cream

My Clarisonic – oh wow.. can't live without

Phone charger

Ariel the Little Mermaid Doll

and my beloved MaliBuBu monkey which was the first
cute bear my boyfriend ever bought me

That's my Surgery bag list.. probably way over
the top but it makes me feel more secure! I'd feel like I'd
forgotten something if I didn't over pack. Like I said.. I
treat my little hospital visits as a mini holiday haha!

Outfit choice for the hospital, in your face,
leopard print leggings to distract from my face with no
makeup on, cute little flats embellished with jewels and a
loose white tee.

So that was it, I was ready. I took my bags to the
car and got in the passenger side. Instantly lit a cigarette,
I needed to, I was starting to freak out. All that was
going through my head was the thought of a colostomy
bag, I kept trying to be positive but it was pretty damn
hard. Again, thank you to everyone who sent me
positive, supportive messages; they helped a lot. We got
stuck behind a number of slow ass drivers but I was
secretly grateful because it was delaying the fact I had
surgery. I had to be at the hospital for 11, but I'm a
Virgo and so is my Mum so we were early, which I

would much rather be so I can get mentally prepared and not feel flustered. We got there and the world's tiniest car park was filling up fast, but luckily there was a slot as soon as we got in and Mum parked the car pretty niftily. She then went to get a car park ticket whilst I lit up yet another cigarette and had a little cry in the car. Mum came back and sat there whilst I finished it and was joking with me asking where my sunglasses were. I knew I'd forgotten something! Joking. Could have done with them though, felt bloody shocking without my makeup and didn't want to bump into anyone I knew!

So we leave the car and begin to head inside and then I just froze and burst into tears and told Mum that I can't do it and I need to go home now. I'll learn to live with the pain, it's okay. She gave me a hug and told me it will all be over soon and started walking me across the road towards the hospital.

We get to the lift and I think I'd started talking absolute crap, like the time I used to be majorly scared of needles (so used to them now) and I had to have an injection at school and I was talking about the time I went to the zoo just to distract myself. Like I talk absolute bullshit when I'm scared. I have no idea what I was going on about to my Mum though. We get up to the 5th floor (ironically, the floor I was born on – well, I was born in theatre technically but back then 5th floor was the delivery suite), where Jasmine Suite is based and all my favourite nurses work! Ah see, I'm talking rubbish again just because I can remember how scared I was! As we get out of the lift and start walking down the corridor, I'm walking incredibly slowly, like I genuinely believe a tortoise would have overtaken me the speed I was going at! I told Mum I would feel a lot calmer if I knew my favourite nurse was working, turns out she was. Talk about that calming me down! We get to the ward reception bay and my bed wasn't quite ready but I didn't care. I was way early, think it was like half 10. We went and sat in the day room until it was ready and then after reading a few magazines and having a chat, a pretty lady walked in with who I assumed to be her partner. She looked as scared as me! After a few minutes, I think I asked her if she was here for surgery too. She said that yes, she was and I told her I was really scared, she agreed telling me she was too! Then she turns and asks me if I'm the woman with the blog? I said that I have a blog, yes! She said oh you are, I was reading your blog last night!

Can we just take a moment here dolls.. This made me SO happy! The lady wasn't having treatment for Endometriosis, she was having something else done (I won't say what, people's privacy etc) but to know that my blog had reached someone! She said it made her feel a bit better knowing she wasn't the only one who was scared. I wanted to tell her it made me feel a bit better knowing she had read my blog, that my blog is actually doing some good! I did see her briefly after the surgery. And I'm sure I asked her her name but jeez I was so petrified that day, her name has totally escaped me (not that I would print it here without her permission anyway!) but it would be really nice if I could remember it. Anyway, she was a really lovely woman and looked amazing even though she was about to have terrifying surgery!

I then hear my name being called to tell me my bed is ready, so Mum comes with me (she did NOT care if she was about to get thrown out, she could see how scared I was. I was totally more scared than my first surgery purely because of the risk of a colostomy bag). She pulls the curtain around my bed and I got changed into the beautiful hospital gowns that they make you wear. I then started getting worried that Mum was going to be told to go, so I said let's go back in the dayroom for a bit!

I began to get quite tired and in pain as I was stressing out, so we went back to my allocated bed. Within a few minutes my consultant turned up and spoke to me about everything and made sure I was okay, made me laugh a few times too. He's brilliant!

I can't remember too much about the order of events for the next bit but I remember just talking with my Mum until I had to have my bloods taken, this was where I had to say bye to my Mum and I got really upset and didn't want her to go.

Shortly after this, the Anaesthetist who would be working alongside my main Anaesthetist (am I even spelling this right?) came to see me and asked me a ton of questions and made sure I was okay. She was brilliant, really went through everything with me and just had a general chat too! Then the main doctor who would be putting me to sleep came to see me and, oh she was just fantastic! Such a cheeky little face and bubbly smile, she really put me at ease.

I vaguely remember being called down to surgery at around half 12 and I was taken down by one of the student nurses, she was really lovely and kept talking to me to keep me calm. When I got down there it was a bit different to the last time I had surgery, perhaps because it was an afternoon surgery? This time I was seated at a little table whilst I had to answer a ton of the same questions I'd been asked upstairs. I don't mind this obviously, it's great to know they do the correct checks! They then left me to it whilst I waited to be called through. Then ANOTHER Anaesthetist came to check my details and introduced herself! I was then taken through and I almost started crying again, just as we walked around the corner at the swinging doors into the 'Going To Sleep room' (sorry guys, I just have no idea what to call it) both consultants were outside the door speaking with the Anaesthetist. I instantly didn't want to cry in front of my surgeons, I didn't want them to think I was a baby haha, how RIDICULOUS right! They said hello and I was in a kind of daydream so I kind of smiled and just carried on walking, my heart was absolutely racing and I was trying to slow my breathing down.

When I got through the doors, it was a room larger than the one I'd been in last time (I must have been in a larger Operating Theatre or something as it was a dual surgery), I was told by a really nice man to get on the bed and get comfy. In the room there was – hang on, let me just count this out... Five Anaesthetist 's in the room, all having a good chat with me and making me laugh. As I lay down on the bed, one of them moved my hair back and said some nice words (I can't quite remember what) as I was crying because I was scared, not like heaving crying, more tears just rolling down my face! Another got me a tissue and said everything was going to be just great. I was in there about 10 minutes just lying down having a chat and things, whilst they put one of those horribly large cannulas into my left hand and then as they were placing that into my hand, a friendly face popped up over the side! It was my Dad's customer (he's a gentleman's hairdresser) who also happened to be an Anaesthetist – he was dressed in a suit and he said, 'My haircut's bloody terrible', which made me laugh and he said he'd just come to check I was okay! I was like I am now. I meant because I'd seen him, it was nice seeing someone I knew!

So then everyone started talking to me at once about how we knew each other and then I'm guessing the Head Anaesthetist, (I have NO idea what the correct term is, I am not medically educated!) walked in with her chirpy voice saying, 'I've been told we have a VIP here and we are to take EXTRA special care of you', I started laughing and didn't really say anything as at this point I was breathing this stuff in slowly through one of those oxygen masks (It probably was oxygen with the stuff they put in to keep you asleep and drowsy) and she was putting something into my cannula. She said Dr So and so has been along and told us all we are to take extra care of you. Now, I have no idea who Dr So and so is but from what I've gathered since he's pretty high up at the hospital and my Dad also cuts HIS hair! So by this point I am so high on the meds I really am starting to drift off which is great because a part of me did think, oh shit what if I'm still awake and yet I can't tell them I'm awake. After this, I honestly don't remember anything else until I woke up… which you know is a good thing haha!

Drifting off to a thoughtless sleep.. No dreams..

Chapter 23
My Second Surgery…Part Two.

I remember hearing someone screaming in pain, everything just a hazy blur. I tried to open my eyes and they're sort of half open, I couldn't quite open them fully, I felt so weak and tired. As I was opening them I realised the person moaning in pain, was me… hmm that wasn't good! I tried to look around me and I vaguely recollect people being around all sides of the bed.

I realised I was in the recovery room.

I don't really remember too well who was actually there around the bed but I do remember seeing the Head Anaesthetist and she was asking me what type of pain I was in and where the pain was; another person in dark green scrubs was telling me everything would be okay and they were just trying to stabilise my pain. My only memories next are of saying I really need a wee, then my consultant popping up at the end of the bed telling me everything would be just fine and I'm doing great (although I was so out of it, it could have been someone else!) I remember him saying to a blonde lady in dark green scrubs how much fluid did she put in and something about a litre and a half in response – again, this could CLEARLY be all in my own head and to this day I still have no idea what the fluid was about.. maybe the IV drip? I'm not sure! Then my consultant disappeared and reappeared and said he was just going to pop a catheter in.. well, at this point I remember crying and saying that I'd never had one before and will it hurt, I'm scared. I then clamped my legs shut and wouldn't let him in! I remember someone saying to me that I had to relax (in a nice way!) and that it wouldn't hurt, not compared to the pain I was having right now. Someone then helped me to put my legs to one side and I remember feeling so terrified. I absolutely HATE hands down in that area, even after all the prodding and poking I've had over the past year, I still can not stand it. I just have a major fear. So it was a struggle for me to put my legs down, I also remember it hurting and all I wanted to do was keep my legs shut. I just remember my consultant smiling at me as I turned my head and asked how long the surgery had taken. 3 hours. Shorter than last time. Then that's it.. I felt pain relief within a minute or so and I must have gone out for the count as I don't remember anything else.

I MUST have been chattering away at some point as a nurse the next day told me I had been asking when I could put my makeup back on. Typical! Last time I was asking for a Nando's.. this time makeup! I don't remember being transferred to my bed on the ward but what I DO remember is seeing my Mum come walking through the ward doors and round to my side of the bed. As my Mum came to give me a hug, my boyfriend was busy putting balloons on my bed. I looked at him and he looked sort of sad.. no, worried? Then I realised, I had an oxygen mask on my face.. that could have been the reason why! I was so happy to see my boyfriend, I literally thought my heart was going to burst out of my chest, seeing my Mum at the same time instantly made me feel not scared and so secure, just knowing that she was there! They both looked so worried and were asking me how I was. I don't really remember saying much just that I was okay.

Mum asked me if I had drank a peppermint tea yet reminding me that I did not want to be in the pain I was in last time from the trapped gas! I said no, I had just woken up. So she went to ask a nurse for some hot water, a nurse then came to see me saying I couldn't have anything to eat or drink yet and I said why not? She said it was because I would be sick. I told her I wouldn't, I'm starving and could quite happily sit here and eat a full on Sunday dinner and be perfectly fine. She didn't look like she believed me, but came back with a small capsule of their peppermint drink. Freaking kidding me? I drank it. Then one of my favourite nurses came into the ward and Mum called her over and I asked, please can I have one of my peppermint tea's, I don't want pain from the gas, it's awful! I ended up getting my own way! I had two of them I think? And no, I wasn't sick. I'm one of the lucky ones.. Anaesthetic doesn't make me feel nauseous like some people can feel.

My boyfriend had placed all these balloons over my bed, explaining he'd tried to get me an Ariel The Little Mermaid balloon but there was no helium at the Trafford Centre! That huge shop and no bloody helium! For those that don't know, Trafford Centre is a HUGE mall. So you'd expect it to have some helium in stock! He then went on to tell me that there was no Ariel dolls in the Disney store! He looked so upset about it! He'd got me a box of Lucky Charms, which is my all time favourite cereal and in the UK it's INCREDIBLY expensive for a box of cereal. He'd also got me a box of

Hello Panda which is so yummy! He then showered me in hugs and kisses which was the best thing in the world ever. I remember my Step-Mum coming to see me with my Dad, and she had got me a Belle Disney Princess balloon.

So I have a few incisions which you always have which a laparoscopy, I have one in my belly button, one either side of my hip bones and one in-between my belly button and my left hip bone. He went in on the same incisions as last time apart from my lower right hip bone incision – this one he had to cut lower down. I also had two miniature dots next to the lower right incision where during surgery, once he had unstuck my right ovary, he suspended it in mid air. A bit like a dream catcher at a doorway, whilst he worked on excising (cutting away) my endometriosis which was all over the right side.

My consultant came around later that evening – I'm sure my Mum and boyfriend were still there.. although I can't quite remember. I'm not too sure what he said exactly – all I recollect is him telling me I was Endometriosis free now, everything he could see, was gone and he was asking if I was okay and that he would speak to me properly in the morning, that I was to get some rest!

Soon enough visiting time was over (it's only an hour in the evening. I'm sure though that my Mum and boyfriend were there earlier!) and I absolutely hated saying bye to my boyfriend. He couldn't come and see me on the Friday evening because there was a rugby game. I was SO upset about this, then I reminded myself.. it could be worse, my boyfriend could be in the army and he may not even have made it for my surgery.

As it happens he's a rugby player and I was lucky enough to have him there when I woke up. I said my goodbyes and I drifted off to sleep. After having a peppermint tea of course! I think during the night I had some oramorph, but I seriously can't remember.. it was a god send having that catheter though, really made a difference compared to my last surgery. I put my headphones in and was speaking to him for ages; we did this every night I was in hospital and after his training sessions! THIS is what sent me off to sleep, knowing he was there for me!

In the morning, they brought round breakfast and yet again, tried making me have a bread roll.. OH MY LIFE. How many times do I have to tell these people that I absolutely do NOT eat bread? Unless its wheat and gluten free.. it causes me pain! I may well be active Endo free now but damn, I wasn't about to risk it!

After breakfast, a nurse came around and removed my catheter – oh my life.. breathe girls! It kind of stung when it came out, but apart from that it was fine. Just felt a bit funny for a few seconds. I then got out of bed – slowly – and gathered my things so I could wash my face, brush my teeth and start my makeup! Once I'd made it back to bed, surprisingly easily actually. It actually occurred to me why.. I had begun to get in pain and then it disappeared whilst I was in the bathroom washing my face. I looked on my chest and realised I had a patch stuck to it just below my collar bone on the right side. I asked the nurse what it was and she told me it was Fentanyl and it was the equivalent of 125mg morphine or something like that, being released into my body. The tab blocks had worn off and the

Fentanyl had kicked in. So THAT explains why I felt pretty great. I genuinely felt like I could get up, and go to work. Let's just say.. thank god I didn't!

I always sit in the hospital bed doing my makeup. Sometimes I have to lie back for a rest because I'm tired. Some of the student nurses came around to have a look at what I was doing, and this was the point one of the nurses told me I was asking about whether I could put my makeup back on when I'd come round from my surgery!

I did see my consultant that day.. and all I can tell you about the surgery is that all my organs were unstuck and all active Endometriosis was removed and I was told a 30% chance of it coming back within so many years. He explained to me that my Endometriosis although it spread during Prostap; luckily it was a steady growth and not Endometriosis that grows at a super fast pace, I am very lucky. I have an appointment with him on the 30th of this month, so I'm going to be taking a notebook to write down everything he did.

My brother came to see me too, he got me the cutest get well card! I have a HUGE selection of Get Well cards from family and friends, which I still have up on my windowsill! My Mum came to see me every visit and my Dad and Step-Mum came in the evenings.

I stayed in hospital until the Saturday, when I finally got to go home. I was staying with my Mum until I was back on my feet again. I couldn't wait to eat loads of food. I had a curry that night.. oh wow, heaven on a plate! It was so good to eat again, after doing the nil by mouth and before that, the awful Low Residue Diet!

I was glued, no stitches at all this time. Last time I was mainly glue and one stitch. My glue also came off a lot faster this time – I still have a little left 18 days later. I ended up itching them and it bled a little. So had to put some little bandage pads over the top so I wouldn't do it.

My boyfriend brought some home from rugby which were brilliant and stuck on but didn't hurt when you peeled them off, but they were super soft.

I spent the next few days after surgery walking around like the hunchback of Notre Dame. My Mum and boyfriend kept reminding me to stand up straight! I was scared though!

That's basically how my surgery went! I must also point out that I began to bleed the day after surgery and I had also had my first period since Prostap on the 6th June.

Positive vibes help aid a speedy recovery.

And rest.

Lots of it.

Chapter 24
Recovery, Recovery, Recovery and a Hospital Appointment

Pain, pain go away.. just don't come back another day.

I didn't realise recovering from a major surgery would actually be that difficult. Naive? Could say that I guess. I mean, sure I had my first laparoscopy in Sept/Oct (why can I STILL not remember the actual month?), but I went onto Prostap pretty much straight away and I was bound to be in pain anyway as Endo had been left behind on my bowel and bladder. So at the time I didn't even think anything of it and it was also Christmas time in my retail job so I had no choice but to just crack on with it. Sick days in December? Only if you're dying. And I mean dying.. like your arm hanging off isn't a good enough reason. This time around, I'm active endo free. Which is why I can't understand why I'm still in pain?

Yes, it's a different pain. It's like dull aches on my right side and a cramping sensation in the middle of my belly. This pain is nothing but it does remind me of the pain I had as a teenager. It still hurts. I'm sick of hearing, 'Oh well, you have no Endometriosis left, it was all cut away.' Yes, there is no Endo there but than five weeks ago I was having a massive operation. Prostap is still leaving my body, I've bled three times for 7 days since surgery. Now fuck off. I'm still exhausted. I don't need your crap medical knowledge because guess what? You have none. They irritate the hell out of me.

This Tuesday just gone, I visited the hospital for what I was hoping would be the last time for a long while. I had my post-op appointment with my consultant. He reassured me about the pains I am getting and explained that everything is just settling down. I asked him about exercise and he told me that yes, I can go ahead and exercise but not to do anything silly. He told me there is a 30% chance of it coming back. So basically I'm thinking if I stay positive it won't come back!

He told me that I wouldn't be being discharged from the hospital and I will be closely monitored for the next 24 months, with regular check-ups. I also have to fill in the Endometriosis survey regularly so they can keep an eye on my health and if anything is awry I will be called in for scans etc. Which is incredibly reassuring.

He then went on to say, if I wasn't planning on any babies soon then I must consider a form of contraception but he didn't push this as he knows I just don't react well to any hormones. So sick of them. I am also not going through a trial and error of bloody contraceptive pills to find out they're all crap and give me spots. No thank you. That's just my decision though. Rather just use a condom than mess with my head anymore that it needs messing with.

I do want to try something for mood swings though, something herbal. Any recommendations will be highly appreciated!

As I was concerned about the amount of times I had bled since surgery, my consultant explained that because of the Prostap and coming off that and then having this major surgery, it was incredibly normal for this to happen. So right now, I'm just keeping track of every bleed and hoping my body settles down into a pattern. I'm praying that 2 periods a month doesn't happen like it did before I first went on the contraceptive pill. I can't afford to be bleeding for that amount of time.

I'm very exhausted today! Do any of you have any ideas for controlling mood swings? Mine are RIDICULOUS.

Back to work next week!

Chapter 25
It really has been far too long.. Period Talk.

Wow, it has been months since I last posted. It has been crazy hectic lately. I'll give you a brief summary of what's been happening just so I can get you all up to

speed and then I can get to the meaty part and vent my emotions.

Since recovering from my surgery, I felt amazing – like I had NEVER ever ever felt so good – okay, maybe before I began my periods, I felt that good! I was working out three times a week for an hour each time (not at the gym, just at home with some weights and a couple of workout shows I'd recorded off the TV), I was getting back in shape. I'd had my first ever PAIN – FREE PERIOD. Do you know how good that FELT? I called my Mum and my best friend to tell them I was on my period and that I was in no pain and I had lots of energy.. yeah sure, I had a few twinges of cramps but FUCK ME! NOTHING AT ALL like what I was used to. I have NEVER had a pain – free period, I'm pretty sure the kind of period I had was a 'normal' period.. those cramps are NOTHING. Like I was jumping out of bed and all sorts. I was AMAZED.. I honestly felt like I had my life back, I had no other pains the rest of the month, I had lots of energy, I felt like ME.

Second period 31 days later. Again, more of the same, I was just so amazed at how little pain I was getting! Both periods lasted my usual 7 days-8 days.

Third period.. I'd started back at work, again another virtually pain free period. I had noticed I was more exhausted than usual though and I know it had nothing to do with being back at work as I did a staged return where I was only working a couple of days a week.

Fourth period. Oh hello mama. This hurt. The whole LEAD up to my period.. HURT. I think the day of my period or possibly the second day (I can not remember), I remember feeling as though I wanted to be sick, I had intense pain, exactly how it was before my very first surgery, I was in so much pain I was screaming yet no-one was at home so who the hell I was screaming for I don't know. My boyfriend wasn't due home for another twenty minutes. I remember I had been taking Tramadol, Paracetamol all day but I couldn't eat anything because I was in too much pain, it MUST have been my second day of my period, argh can't remember! I crawl out of bed to make it to the toilet, the last thing I remember is sitting there and then I woke up in bed.

According to my boyfriend, he had come home from work and Teddy had jumped on him and ran upstairs to the bathroom, my boyfriend had found me on the floor and I was shaking and my eyes were all funny. He got me onto the bed and apparently I was speaking but not making sense. He rang my Mum (who's a nurse) and she told him he needed to give me a sugary drink so that's what he did. All I remember is being put on the phone to my Mum and her asking if I had eaten anything. I told her no and she said that's why I had passed out. I was meant to be going on holiday the day after! I've never seen my boyfriend look so worried, it actually scared me!

Has anyone else ever passed out on their period? I used to do it a lot but not to the point where I would be physically shaking and slurring my words.

Long story short, ever since that horrific period I have been in pain almost every day. I don't understand what the hell is going on. I am so frustrated, I wish I could just SEE inside my body.

I managed to go on holiday (yuck, periods on holiday) and I know this sounds crazy but it's like the hot weather made my bleeding minimal.. I've never had anything like it! I was in AGONY but my bleeding was minimal. But I was in pain for a solid 7 days. Luckily I managed to enjoy my holiday towards the end, but I was just so exhausted. It was a very relaxing holiday though.

Before I go on to tell you about my next period (my most recent) I better catch you all up to speed with what's been going on in my life! Basically, I went back to work and then a few weeks later, I handed in my notice. We were moving! As you know, my boyfriend plays rugby, he decided he wanted to go back and play rugby union so he left the team he was playing for up north and signed for a team further south. It meant we had to leave and relocate – new jobs, new house. Everything. Stressful right? Yeah.. the whole reason why I haven't written anything recently. Things have been crazy busy. So we have moved almost three hours away and I've only just managed to secure myself a job I want. I have been offered three different jobs since I've been here but the money they were offering.. I wasn't getting myself out of bed for that. I know it sounds ungrateful, but I've done the job I do for 5 years+ I deserved a lot more than what they could pay me. Anyway, I accepted a job yesterday and I can't wait to start, I am so excited about it! We have also just managed to find the most perfect place to live! All in a days work hey. It's only taken a month.. grr! I wish it had all been sorted much sooner but better late than never. We move in this weekend so at least that is those stresses gone. I still have a money stress.. I acquired quite a bit of debt whilst I was off sick for so long.. SSP is awful, it really is. Seriously can't wait to begin work and get my money back on track. I need to look into some kind of work insurance or something – if there is such a thing, so if I had to have that much time off again then I would be able to y'know.. live.

Onto my most recent period. For the past few weeks we have been staying with my boyfriend's parents. In the lead up to my period, I was in agony, my moods were all over the place. My ovaries were on fire, I could feel them swelling into big hot balls of fire. It was hell. Sheer hell. Back pain. Shoulder pain. Neck pain. Leg pain. Vagina pain. Ovary pain. And then this twisting, ache as though a little man was inside my pelvic area and he'd decided to put a few pictures up on the surrounding walls. It felt like a dull thud. Disgusting.

My painkillers weren't working. Oramorph wasn't touching it. I was getting stressed because I was so far away from MY hospital and MY doctors. I ended up at the emergency doctors as a temporary resident – I refuse to register at a doctors down here.. it took me over

12 years to finally get my GP right, I wasn't changing that for the world. The female doctor that I saw was HOPELESS.

'Oh, I get pain when I'm ovulating too, I know what it's like'

Have you got Endometriosis too?

'No'

Oh okay well, just to give you a brief history, I was diagnosed with Endometriosis, I had a 15cm by 12cm complex Endometrioma removed from my left ovary plus extensive excision. Then went on to have a further surgery to remove from my bowel and bladder and then to remove the Endometriosis that had spread all over my right side due to Prostap pissing it off.

'What's Prostap'

A chemically induced menopause.

'Oh well I don't think it will have grown back, Endometriosis stays away once it has been removed. I think the Oramorph you have been taking is too strong and you should try just Paracetamol and Ibuprofen'

Thanks, bye.

So this proves my point as to why I won't register at another doctors anywhere. I don't trust them.

Oh shit, did I mention she gave me a pregnancy test? Lady.. it would be a damn fucking miracle if that had happened. I also couldn't be bothered to set her straight – it was 10pm and I just wanted to go home at this point. I just wanted my Mum. Don't get me wrong, my boyfriend was there the entire time, he's my absolute strength!

I got on with my week of hell.

This pretty much brings us up to the current day. I started getting pains again yesterday, I've been getting them on and off since my last period. I can't lie on my right hand side. My ovaries are swollen – well, it bloody feels like it I look pregnant but I'm not. My Mum made me call my consultant at the hospital a few weeks ago, and I have an appointment on the 26th to see him. I just have to hold out until then. I can do this. Done it for long enough in the past.

I am apprehensive though. What if I just get dismissed? My consultant is not the kind of doctor who would do that but there's always that voice in the back of my head that says 'What if?', just because of all my previous experiences. What if it isn't back and this is just my normal? I've spoken to the other girls who had their surgery around same time as me and they're in the same position. They're in pain again. I guess, only time will tell.

Oh, I'm due on next week too, might throw a period party. It's that fun, right?

Sorry for the rant, it's not actually THAT long really. I have summarised this a hell of a lot. I won't bore you anymore.

Apprehensive about my appointment…

Chapter 26
My Pain Today.

I'm in pain.

I'm trying to distract myself but it's not working well.

My legs are heavy and sharp.
My back feels like I have a machete wedged inside.
I am so nauseous, my body aches all over, I'm lay down but feel abnormally dizzy as though someone, some bastard is pushing me from side to side, see-sawing me over barbed wire, pulling and tearing it across my abdomen.

My belly is carrying a sack of bricks inside a bag of numb cotton wool. I tried to stand earlier and felt like my insides were going to burst out of my body. I had to hold my belly, if I didn't I feared my womb would push out of my belly button.
My hips are superglued to the mattress, the fucking pain in my shoulder is back. I am so sick and tired of all this.

I'm done with it all. I have had enough.

I don't know where all you amazing women with Endometriosis get the strength but I fucking can't carry on like this.

I had two months pain free.

Pain free.

It was bliss, heaven, more than I can wish for. I don't want billions of pounds in the bank, sure it would be nice, but I just want to be PAIN-FREE. I've experienced it, it was the best time of my life. Like before I'd hit puberty. I felt free.

Now I feel robbed.

I have moved to an amazing new home but what good is it when I'm stuck in the bedroom unable to move, again.

Did I mention my fucking vagina hurts? It hurts so badly. The fuck does that happen for?

I can't stop crying, I need to find some fucking strength. But right now I'd rather be dead than go through all this bullshit again. I'm sick of it, I can't get past this today.

I'm sorry for being weak.

I just think I've been strong long enough now and I haven't got the energy anymore to deal with this.

Please someone just find a fucking cure, I beg you. Please, you have to stop this pain for everyone worldwide.

I'm sick and tired of being tortured by my own body.

I have no choice though, I have to stay strong..
Tired.

Chapter 27

I had my appointment, I had to keep a pain diary until I next saw him so we could talk about the next options as I really shouldn't have been in pain.

A lot happened in between these two appointments.

It turns out I was pregnant. Me, pregnant. Shocked, completely and utterly shocked.

I told my consultant at the follow up appointment and he jumped for joy and brought my nurse into the room who also did the same. They were all cheering and shouting to the other members of staff to come into the room. People in the waiting room must have been confused as to what was going on.

To this day I still can't believe it.

Later that year I gave birth to a beautiful baby boy. My pregnancy was horrific and the journey after I had him wasn't so pretty either. To this day I still can't believe that this happened. The pain that I was feeling must have been my body healing but the movements that started to create my baby must have been causing additional pain. It was an incredibly painful pregnancy but I was oh so grateful. I am so completely and utterly in love with him. Now I hope my endometriosis doesn't ever rear its ugly head again. I have to stay positive that it will leave me alone.

37222879R00070

Printed in Great Britain
by Amazon